Advance Praise

"For over a decade you have taught me significant lessons in leadership and in life and this book is no exception. By sharing your journey in this thought-provoking book, you've given us all a road map that can help each of us draw closer to God. This insightful book will challenge and inspire all who read it to integrate Jesus into every aspect of our lives, so that we too, will be victorious in spite of life's challenges."

—**Connie Reinhardt**, CPA/CFF, CFE, Member with
Myers and Stauffer Accounting

"*Lost & Restored* brings the heart of the Father, through Suzanne's own personal journey and her counseling practice, to minister to everyone who reads her book. It is a heartfelt journey to ongoing wholeness that everyone can relate to.

She brings experience, practical tools and proven models for emotional healing. Jesus is the only one who can heal and she does a wonderful job leading us to Him, the Good Shepherd and Great Physician."

—**Sylvia Wright**, SMASH Ministry leader (Soul, Mind, and Spirit Healing) at Bridgeway Church in Denver, Colorado

"Scripture teaches that God has provided many ways to be healed: *'God has appointed in the church...miracles then gifts of healings'* (1 Cor. 12:28). One of these gifts is inner healing, another is deliverance, another is energy psychology. There are many various tools our Heavenly Father has given in order for us to be made well!

Several of these methods are mentioned in this book, *Lost & Restored*, as Suzanne Simpson shares her personal journey to freedom through the counsel of the Wonderful Counselor Himself. Truly we comfort others with the comfort we ourselves have received, and it is fully available to all of us in Christ (2 Cor. 1:3–5). Invite Jesus into the broken places of your life today and let His love transform and heal you from the inside out."

—**Dr. Charity Virkler Kayembe**, Coauthor of *Hearing God through Your Dreams: Understanding the Language God Speaks at Night* and *EFT for Christians: Tapping into God's Peace and Joy*

"Suzanne Simpson's new book, *Lost & Restored*, gives the reader a picture into her journey and her heart for the Body of Christ to be like sheep that are led by the Good Shepherd, who leads them out of the dark and scary places of life and into the safe and beautiful sheepfold of life. She openly shares her own struggles and doubts and then offers her journey of how she moved out of pain into healing and restoration. She also created insightful reflection questions at the end of each chapters to take the reader from information into a transformational experience. Finally, she offers a pathway at the end of the book that offers next steps to enter into a full restoration process. The cover entices us into this journey...pick it up and get started."

—**Tamara J Buchan**, Author of *Identity Crisis: Reclaim the True You* and *You were Meant for More* Series, Founder and Director of Reclaim Initiative, www.ReclaimInitiative.com.

"*Lost and Restored* is both profound and pragmatic. Suzanne includes her own vulnerable stories of being lost and restored as well giving her husband, Les, an opportunity to share his raw healing journey stories — which I found both refreshing and connecting. In addition to having deep spiritual truths, this book is easy to read and I found myself curled up by my fireplace each evening looking forward to the next chapter. In a very unobtrusive way, Suzanne is able to invite the reader into practical healing applications through her own probing and honest journey. This is a great resource for anyone, anywhere who has ever felt lost and longs to be fully restored."

—**Laura Greiner**, PHD. Heart Sync Minister

"*Lost & Restored* offers a warm, intimate description of the Father's love touching the secret places of the heart. With personal examples woven throughout, Suzanne gives the reader accessible instruction in bringing our daily needs to the Lord. A wonderful read!"

—**Sarah J. Thiessen**, LMFT, LPC Director of the
Splankna Therapy Institute

Lost and Restored

LOST AND RESTORED

Healing Your
Heart with
the Father

SUZANNE B. SIMPSON

NASHVILLE

NEW YORK • LONDON • MELBOURNE • VANCOUVER

Lost and Restored

Healing Your Heart with the Father

Published in New York, New York, by Morgan James Publishing. Morgan James is a trademark of Morgan James, LLC. www.MorganJamesPublishing.com

ISBN 9781642797619 paperback
ISBN 9781642797626 eBook
Library of Congress Control Number: 2019948556

Cover Design by:
Megan Dillon
megan@creativeninjadesigns.com

Interior Design by:
Christopher Kirk
www.GFSstudio.com

Disclaimer: Although every precaution has been taken to verify the accuracy of the information contained herein, the author and publisher assume no responsibility for any errors or omissions. No liability is assumed for damages that may result from the use of information contained within.

** The names of clients referred to in this book have been changed to protect their identities, and their experiences are recounted with their permission.

Morgan James is a proud partner of Habitat for Humanity Peninsula
and Greater Williamsburg. Partners in building since 2006.

Get involved today! Visit
MorganJamesPublishing.com/giving-back

To my husband Les, for modeling to me a deep personal connection to the Lord. He faithfully encourages me to break through my resistance and allow God to work in me.

I am especially grateful to the Lord for walking me through the insights I have shared here—the vulnerable areas that may help others heal like I experienced. I am thankful that I have a true Father who showers His constant love on me far beyond what I can comprehend.

I am dedicating this to the reader who is seeking an avenue to receive the peace and joy that is available to you as you fully receive the redemption of your soul.

The Spirit of the Lord is upon Me, Because He has anointed Me to preach the gospel to the poor; He has sent Me to heal the brokenhearted, To proclaim liberty to the captives And recovery of sight to the blind, To set the liberty to those who are oppressed; To proclaim the acceptable year of the Lord. (Luke 4:16-19)

Contents

Introduction

During my years of experience as a psychotherapist assisting with people's emotional struggles, I have come to understand that the main path to healing and wholeness is through Christ, who was God's perfect sacrifice—the Lamb of God. Because of that unblemished sacrifice, we can offer ourselves to God with all our blemishes and receive healing.

Over the years, I've searched for healing methods that can truly release us from the bondage of our emotional traumas. In the process, I've discovered that we can't do it without the help of the power available to us through God. We can trust Him for our healing rather than trusting in man's philosophies that often do little to restore us to health. Through the pages of this book, I am hoping to open your eyes to the incredible love and healing potential we can access through the person of Christ.

Scripture often depicts humans as sheep—an apt metaphor. Sheep are easily led astray and need a shepherd to protect and rescue them. In the same way, we need a Good Shepherd who will pursue us and restore our brokenness, so that we may live vibrant, Spirit-directed lives.

Throughout scripture we see God's deep desire to restore us to the place where we can truly be light to the world of darkness—a world that is desperately in need of a Savior for guidance and healing. My greatest desire is to encourage you to participate in an ongoing relationship with Christ that leads to transformation. Without that kind of breakthrough healing, we can become dry wells with very little water of the spirit to offer others.

Within this book, you will discover some out-of-the-box counseling methods, tools, and encouragement from my own healing journey, the journey of my husband, Les Simpson, and the testimonies of others who have experienced powerful methods of transformation.

Take out your journal and get ready for a self-discovery journey where you can examine yourself in a deeper way. Each chapter provides soul-searching questions at the end that allow you to deepen the exploration of yourself.

Chapter One
Cracking the Wall

He who has the bride is the bridegroom; the friend
of the bridegroom, who stands and hears him,
rejoices greatly at the bridegroom's voice;
therefore, this joy of mine is now full.
—John 3:29

On September 11, 2001, I sat rooted in front of my television set, shaken by a horrific event none of us had ever imagined. I watched in horror, seeing smoke billowing from the top of one of the towers as a commercial plane hit our very own Twin Towers in New York City. My mind raced with questions—how was this even possible? My heart beat faster as I tried to make sense of what I was seeing. Who were the enemies that suddenly invaded our country? Was the United States really under attack by unknown terrorists? Would we live on the edge of fear and dread from that moment on? Would we ever feel safe again? Had the heritage which our forefathers so desperately fought for been destroyed in a matter of hours?

I took a deep breath. What would this mean for our country? What would it mean for me as I prepared for my long-awaited wedding in two weeks? I looked away from the television and suddenly felt panic rising. Soon, relatives began to call saying they would not be comfortable traveling. The flowers ordered from overseas wouldn't be coming after all. And my brother who was overseas wouldn't be there to give me away at my wedding. I was overwhelmed by feelings of disappointment and sadness. I had waited fifty years to find and marry the man of my dreams, and now it would be marred by a horrific event over which I had no control.

Momentarily my attention returned to the television screen, and I felt guilty realizing others were suffering far more than I. It occurred to me that we might need to postpone the wedding; I wondered how anyone could come and rejoice with two people joining in holy matrimony when the rest of the world was grieving.

I was torn regarding where to focus my attention—on my wedding plans or clients traumatized by such a stunning catastrophe. The phone immediately began to ring in my psychotherapy office with calls from individuals who suddenly felt personally at-risk and vulnerable. The tragedy also brought to light past events that made them feel unsafe due to circumstances beyond their control. Some carried deep emotional scars that they had buried, hoping they would never surface again.

I became aware that our country would never be the same again. What had once felt like a safe place was no longer safe at all. My little wedding appeared very insignificant in light of the bigger picture. The lyrics from "America the Beautiful" began to race through my mind. I remembered the repetitive theme: "God shed his grace on thee." That left a question: Had God lifted His hand of protection from a rebellious nation that no longer saw the need for Him in our culture, our schools or the affairs of our government? Or had God allowed it to reveal our tremendous need for Him in a world that had become spiritually distant?

When traumatic events occur, I always draw on this comforting truth: Our God is able and eager to wrap us in His peace no matter how tough our challenges become. He knows every emotion in my heart. If I just call out to him and honestly share my fears and concerns, He is right there in the moment to share my pain and anguish.

On that fateful day when the towers fell, I rushed to God and wept uncontrollably, broken and traumatized that such a thing could occur in our precious America. In my deep grief, I felt His loving arms embrace me and shower me with endless love and the reassurance that He would never leave or forsake me. I was amazed by the way He walked with me through those next two weeks with the comfort that only a loving Father could give.

Then He revealed an even deeper remarkable truth: that my marriage was really about allowing myself to be the bride of Christ, my true bridegroom, and that my husband was a physical companion sent to walk with me through this journey we call life. The movies certainly don't portray that concept. Filmmakers always tend to promote fickle romantic love, implying that if we don't have that type of relationship, it must not be true love, when the exact opposite is reality.

Even the vows we wrote reflected the idea that I was choosing Les as my physical companion to walk with me spiritually through life. Could I embrace this concept and live it out? That would be determined over the following years of married life. Even though God had clearly revealed this to me, He left me to walk it out. Somehow, I realized that I needed to die daily to the desire for my physical husband to give me the value I was forever seeking. I could only get that kind of confirmation from God.

After being single for many years, I thought I had learned to depend on God. I had imagined Him being right there beside me when I felt awkward going to parties alone or spending time with married couples. But now that God had blessed me with a husband I would need to trust for something new, that He would still be there to guide, support and comfort me.

As I reflect on what 9-11 has shown me, I am aware that we all have hidden terrorists within us, waiting to attack and reveal themselves at inopportune times when we least expect them. These terrorists may show up as bursts of uncontrollable anger that surface before we lash out at someone. We may wonder how we can experience such violent reactions to situations that don't seem to justify that magnitude of feelings.

The Psalmist David was portrayed in scripture as a man of such contrasts. He had a heart after God, but at the same time, his life was a picture of rebellious, sin-ridden behavior that left him facing unimaginably challenging consequences. He lamented with God over his anxious thoughts and asked God to show him what was in his innermost being. "Search me, O God, and know my heart: try me and know my anxieties." (Psalm 139:23) He wanted God to reveal what was hidden deep in his heart so he could find restoration in a God who wanted to heal and deliver him. It took great courage to ask that of God. I believe that was why he was considered a man after God's own heart.

It's no wonder that David's psalms continually asked God to protect him from his enemies. In fact, he was probably aware that his inner struggles were a much greater threat than many of his human enemies, because evil internal drives and addictions led him into deeper bondage to sin.

David's life proves the point that it's easy to fall into sinful behavior, until we've corrected wrong thinking and misbeliefs that lead us away from God who is always there, ready to restore us. "Like sheep, they are led to the grave, where death will be their shepherd. In the morning, the godly will rule over them. Their bodies will rot in the grave, far from their grand estates. But as for me, God will redeem my life. He will snatch me from the power of death." (Psalm 49:14-15, NLT) David describes us like sheep headed toward ultimate destruction and eternal separation from God. Fortunately, God has shattered the death sentence that hangs over our heads, so we can live abundantly, once we invite Him into our lives. We all need a Shepherd who will guide us and lead us into all truth, bringing redemption and healing to our souls.

Sheep are repeatedly mentioned in scripture—around 500 times! By studying the character of sheep, I discovered that they are desperately in need of someone to lead them. Apart from the Good Shepherd, it's easy for us, like sheep, to be led astray by desires that lure us to indulge our insatiable appetites. In fact, the devil's greatest enticement is to give us what we think we want.

Humility vs. Pride

There is a movie based on a popular novel by Thomas Hardy entitled *Far from the Madding Crowd*. The movie tells the story of a sheep rancher who lost his whole flock of sheep when an untrained, unruly dog led them astray. The sheep were led off a cliff into a valley of death, leaving the rancher without a penny. Even though it seems the rancher lost everything, in the end, because of his humility, he regained what he longed for: the heart of the woman he loved.

Like the sheep that followed an untrained sheep dog, we too can be led astray. How often are we lured toward some shiny object that promises to make our lives complete, but leaves us feeling betrayed and even worse, in debt? Only when we humble ourselves and admit that we seek value out of pride, can the Lord open our eyes to true fulfillment.

Perhaps we're seeking power, glory or money that comes as an angel of light to offer us exactly what we think we want. We may think: "If only I get that promotion or my business grows by leaps and bounds, making me rich." Or, "If only I can find a husband to give me the security and respect for which I long. "If only my children win great honors in school about which I can boast, I will feel valuable." When we're motivated by those things, we define internal value with temporal things, leaving us void of the true identity we can only find in a relationship with Father God.

When Adam and Eve heard the voice of the Lord, they "hid themselves from the presence of the LORD God among the trees of the garden." (Genesis 3:8) They were spiritually dead and hid out of shame, once their fellowship with God was broken due to Eve's pride and desire to become like God. From then on, the Levitical law required people to offer an unblemished lamb as a sacrifice for sin.

Under the new covenant, Christ died, replacing animal sacrifices once and for all. We can now receive Christ as the covering that erases our sin so that God remembers it no more.

Thus, the downward spiral toward spiritual death is reversed, and He gives us life! However, the soul work that enables our intimate connection with Christ requires humility. We must set aside our pride and, like David, ask God to search our minds and hearts to reveal our areas of weakness and brokenness. It's only when we allow God in to address our issues that we can receive His healing and restoration.

We're all tainted in some way, requiring deliverance from our prideful nature. Much like King David, we seek to get our value from external things. In my own life, I've found that when I try to find my value in doing and being certain things, I am left dissatisfied and unfulfilled. I am left far short of what Christ wants to give me—the reassurance that I am fully loved as I am, without the need to perform. It's a gift He's given me! What a blessing it is to know that I am loved no matter what.

The Foundation We Build On

Once we've humbled ourselves and allowed Christ to reveal those areas where we've gone astray, we may find that our inner foundation is structurally weak and prone to failure. Anyone involved in the construction industry knows that people need to consider the quality of the soil on which they build if they want the structure to endure the test of time. Has the foundation been built to shift with the soil—the ebbs and flows of the environment? Or, is it a solid cement slab that doesn't consider external variables? Cracks can form in both types if they aren't built to last.

When I was in my late twenties, I decided to purchase my first home on the meager salary I was making in the retail field. After I had gone through escrow, my Dad came to see the home and quickly found that it was leaning to one side and might have some foundation problems. In addition to foundation problems, I later discovered that a ceiling beam in the living room had been removed, causing the front wall of the house to slope toward the street! Through that ordeal I learned a very important life lesson—that we need a firm foundation and the structural integrity of every part to sustain us over a lifetime.

To thrive the way God intended, we need a healthy foundation in spirit, soul, and body. "May the God of peace himself sanctify you completely; may your whole spirit, soul, and body be preserved blameless at the coming of the Lord Jesus Christ." (1 Thessalonians 5:23) God wants to work in these areas. However, the soul tends to be the most deeply affected, since it demands that we examine ourselves for things we have held onto throughout our lives to our detriment. Even though our spirit is made new in Christ, there are deeper hurts in our souls that keep us from living life to the fullest.

Many people don't see themselves as God sees them—believing lies that have convinced them they are unworthy or insignificant. Others are bitter, refusing to forgive, and stay in bondage to a spirit of anger. Or they may have a strong will that refuses to let anyone control them. While that's not necessarily a bad thing, it can prevent them from humbling themselves to allow Christ to touch the deep wounds that impact the way they see and respond to the world around them. Christ was always very clear when He posed the question: "Do you want to be healed?" (John 5:6) The choice is ours. He's waiting for us to admit that we need Him because we're unable to address our own issues and allow His love and healing to bring new freedom and great joy that's found only in Him. What a great God He is!

Embracing Healing

The Merriam-Webster Dictionary defines the word "blemish" as a verb this way: "to hurt or damage the good condition of (something)", or as a noun: "a mark that makes something imperfect or less than beautiful." We all have imperfections, but we can be healed of the scars of past hurts imprinted on our souls.

These scars affect the life energy running throughout our bodies that God breathed into us in the beginning. When we hold onto negative thoughts, memories, and trauma over the years, the vital life energy gets blocked. Once it's stored in negative thought patterns, it has a way of impacting our lives in many ways, most of them counterproductive. I struggle to understand why we refuse to believe that our energy and outlook can be affected by hidden negative emotions.

We often bury negative emotions, thinking they will somehow magically disappear. But while we may have suppressed them, locking them up beyond our conscious awareness, they can still raise their ugly heads when we least expect them. In fact, research shows that more than 95 percent of emotions are subconscious. These emotions are a lifelong accumulation of events that left marks we try to ignore, including such things as the loss of a family member, being bullied in elementary school, false perceptions about our worth, or abuse of one kind or another. The beliefs that create such emotions can produce a destructive frequency within the cells of the body. No matter how deeply they're buried they impact many areas of our lives including finances, health, and most importantly, our relationships with God and others.

In the same way, the trauma of 9-11 acted as a trigger that brought up earlier events, provoking feelings of danger and fear for many citizens. The soul and body remembered those previous at-risk feelings as if the past events were happening in the present. This process bypasses the rational brain, accessing the reactive part of the brain that responds as if the same feeling is being activated now. At this point our ability to rationally think through a situation is greatly impaired, leaving us feeling confused and unable to live the life we want. These emotions can feel far more overwhelming than the situation warrants and lead to all kinds of anxieties. If we can trace the emotional triggers back to the origin of the memories, we stand a good chance to clear out the root and heal.

> **Pain is a good thing because it connects us more deeply to the inner struggles that God wants to bring to light.**

Not long ago I was lying in bed when I glanced up and saw a cobweb dangling from the ceiling. In that moment, I realized something I hadn't noticed before: I had to be lying down on the bed to see it. If I walked into the room, it wouldn't even be visible. We don't tend to see those inner cobwebs inside us until it's time for God to reveal them through circumstances that trigger the pain. I love what British novelist C.S. Lewis says: "Pain insists upon being attended to. God whispers to us in our pleasures, speaks in our consciences, but shouts in our pains. It is his megaphone to rouse a deaf world." Pain is a good thing because it connects us more deeply to the inner struggles that God wants to bring to light. He can then be the Good Shepherd who leads us to a place of resolution.

Here are some soul-searching questions you will want to explore. Each chapter will include these opportunities.

Soul Searching:

1. Replay your wedding in your mind. If never married, imagine yourself ready to be joined in matrimony. Instead of your spouse, picture Jesus waiting there to greet you. Notice Him looking at you with eyes of adoration, ready to be united with all the beauty He sees in you. How does it feel to be joined to the bridegroom who will always love you unconditionally and never leave you even after death? Knowing that your true marriage is to Christ whether you are single or married, describe how you can look to Him as your partner emotionally and spiritually.

2. When have you been triggered by circumstances that deeply affected your emotions? Was it bigger than the

circumstance merited? If so, what were the emotions you experienced and how did they lead you to a place of deeper pain?

3. Look at some of the cracks in your foundation that might show up as internal blemishes—a lack of self-worth, anger, resentment, or unforgiveness. What are some of the cracks the Lord wants to reveal to you?

Chapter Two

The Good Shepherd

I am the good shepherd, and I know those
that are mine, and I am known by my own.
—John 10:14 (NKJV)

I grew up wondering how other little girls could eagerly jump on their fathers' laps and feel so special and loved. I longed to have the kind of dad who treasured me and embraced me with an excitement that only a loving father can give his kids. Instead, my dad came home exhausted after spending most of his energy working as a busy obstetrician-gynecologist. He worked erratic hours, delivering babies at night, and seeing patients during the day. My dad had very little time or energy left for me at the end of the day. He regularly zoned out for hours in front of the TV without an inkling that his daughter was silently crying out for love and attention. I grew increasingly jealous of the television because it seemed to take precedence over any connection I had with my dad.

When I came to discover that God could be the loving father I longed for, many of those unmet childhood wounds began to heal. As a new Christian, I had a surge of hope and excitement about our newfound relationship. I began to trust and prayed often for His help to surrender every area of my life one by one. I knew that He had an intricate and purposeful plan that would become clear as I drew near and followed His lead. The plan didn't entirely unfold as I had expected, but it did accomplish the work He wanted to do within me, helping me release all kinds of pent-up feelings—many regarding my father's unavailability.

Through trials with failing health, marriage issues and the loss of a career that had validated my abilities, I realized that God was lovingly walking me through these challenges. I began to see how He had sustained me, which drew me even closer. He also began to wean me away from areas where I felt self-sufficient. When I had nothing else to cling to, I began to see the enormity of His love for me as He led me through the healing process. It was very reassuring to know that He hadn't left me without support on my journey.

Orphaned Heart vs. Sonship

In John 14:18 Christ said, "I will not leave you orphans. I will come to you." Though it's the farthest thing from the truth, many of us feel like orphans abandoned by God. In that place, our hearts are tightly sealed up and never can fully receive His unconditional love. In his book entitled *Experiencing Father's Embrace*, author and pastor Jack Frost said that we may continually feel that we must perform for God's love or work to earn His favor.[2] "The orphan spirit causes one to live life as if he does not have a safe and secure place in the Father's heart. He feels he has no place of affirmation, protection, comfort, belonging, or affection. Self-oriented, lonely, and inwardly isolated, he has no one from whom to draw Godly inheritance. Therefore, he has to strive, achieve, compete, and earn everything he gets in life. It easily leads to a life of anxiety, fears, and frustration."

Even though we are born into physical families, we enter this world as orphans lacking the true inheritance that we can have as sons and daughters. We typically don't understand that we are truly loved and bought at an enormous cost to be adopted by the King! No longer are we left to be controlled by earthly fathers who were unable to love us unconditionally. In a generation of broken homes and fathers that may have been unavailable, God has a backup plan. We can replace the orphan heart, filling it with the perfect love of the Father who cradles us in His arms and never leaves us.

> We enter this world as orphans lacking the true inheritance that we can have as sons and daughters.

An orphan spirit can cause us to live rigid, performance-based lives, with no lasting joy or peace, because the emptiness is never filled. Much like the Pharisees of Jesus' days, we value obedience to laws rather than the warmth of relationship. (Galatians 5:1 NAS) says: "It was for freedom that Christ has set us free; therefore, keep standing firm and do not be subject again to a yoke of slavery." That yoke of slavery can show up in many ways. When we don't know who God is and the worth He has imparted to us, we strive to be worthy enough. That orphan spirit can reveal itself in many ways, including perfectionism, comparison, lack of assertiveness/self-confidence, rejection, and/or failing to walk in the love of the Good Shepherd. Listed below are the characteristics that we need to understand if we are to embrace His love.

Characteristics of a Good Shepherd

- **He Continually Guides Us**

Phillip Keller shares in his book *The Shepherd Looks at Psalm 23* that sheep need a great deal of guidance as they move from pasture to pasture so that they remain free of parasites.[3] This process helps keep the pastures free from overgrazing and soil erosion so that they don't develop ruts and desert wastes. When sheep are poorly managed and not handled with intelligent care, they can be subject to the whims of their own destructive habits.

Doesn't this describe us and the reason we need to follow a good shepherd? We too, like sheep, can be led astray, toward our wayward desires. "We all like sheep have gone astray; we have turned, everyone, to his own way. And the Lord has laid on Him the iniquity of us all." (Isaiah 53:6)

- **He is Forgiving and Loves Unconditionally**

I wonder where I would be if I were left to my willful, sin-ridden ways... If I didn't believe that Father God could be that good, available father that I longed to be loved by... If I never believed that when I screwed up, He would be there to receive me with open, forgiving arms... If I never realized that He could comfort me during times of stress. The story of the prodigal son comes to mind here. Even when the son lost his inheritance and found himself in disgrace, his father still welcomed him with open arms and love that was forgiving and unconditional.

A popular praise song describes the Father as good and perfect. I've often thought of those words, pondering that phrase. I know that the word "good" doesn't always mean we get exactly what we long for, but rather describes a shepherd who can continually renew and restore, producing deep inner fruit in our hearts and lives, keeping us on course toward what is best for us. The word "perfect" is defined as complete and lacking nothing.

- **He Doesn't Judge Us on Performance**

Many people I talk to struggle, believing they must perform for God and do it perfectly, as if they must earn His grace. For example, if I gave you the gift of my watch, but then said you had to run two laps around the block, the watch would become something you had to earn. What if I freely gave you the watch with no strings attached? Isn't that what the Good Shepherd wants to give His sheep? Think of it this way: whatever we lack, He is. He wants to restore and complete us, and we can never do enough to earn it! We just need to submit to His leading. Scripture says: "Therefore we conclude that a man is justified by faith apart from the deeds of the law." (Romans 3:28)

- **He Cleanses Us of Impurities**

Shepherds clean sheep regularly to kill the parasites and other infections that create scabs commonly found around their heads.

To get rid of these infections, good shepherds take great care to treat them, dipping sheep in linseed oil mixed with medicinal chemicals to abort the growth of the blemishes. I believe this is what the psalmist David meant when he wrote, "Thou anointest my head with oil." This illustrates our need for a Good Shepherd who is responsible for cleansing us and providing for all our needs.

During summer months, sheep can be especially susceptible to a highly contagious disease that causes microscopic parasites to spread throughout the flock by direct contact between infected and non-infected animals. When two sheep rub heads, the infection spreads from one to another. Once again, the remedy is linseed oil applied to their heads. Before long, when the parasites die the sheep begin to lie down and become more amiable and peaceful. This clearly depicts the way we are easily infected by others' beliefs, attitudes, and values that can afflict us every day.

The media, co-workers, and family members all influence the attitudes that we take on from our environment. Today such attitudes are so prevalent that we see a world filled with hate, backbiting and dissension and violence. The only thing that can comfort us and keep our minds clean is dipping in the anointing oil mentioned earlier by the psalmist David. He shares this poignant statement: "You become my delicious feast even when my enemies dare to fight. You anoint me with the fragrance of your Holy Spirit, you give me all I can drink of you until my heart overflows." (Psalm 23:5, TPT) When we allow ourselves to be anointed or saturated in the oil of the Lord, we can be victorious over our thought life and "simply believe what He says about us."

When sheep rub heads with each other, it's much like the infected relationships we have with others. It can show up in codependent relationships where we're too dependent on each other, and our boundaries get blurred. We may look to that person to meet too many of our emotional needs rather than turning to God. We can also form unhealthy attachments which are called ungodly soul ties. These soul ties can be formed from boundary violations such as sexual relationships outside of marriage, feelings of resentment that keep us bound to others, generational strongholds, and overly attached emotional connections to parents or spouses. Through prayer, we can take responsibility by asking the Lord to sever these ties, so we are no longer attached to people in unhealthy ways.

Why is it that we don't recognize God as the Good Shepherd we so desperately need to fill us up? We may be going through deep trials wondering: where is God, and why am I experiencing so much pain? We may think He has abandoned us and not see the growth—the beautiful design He is weaving into the fabric our life.

- **He Can Lead Us Through the Valleys**

A Good Shepherd is always on the alert for weather changes and storms or predators that might prey on his sheep. Psalm 23:4 (TPT) says: "Lord, even when your path takes me through the valley of deepest darkness, fear will never conquer me, for you already have; For You are with me." The shepherd keeps his eye out for danger as he leads the sheep through a valley. He knows that when a storm comes, it could quickly wash out his entire flock in a matter of minutes.

God is not distant when we are going through the storms of life. He is watching over us with His loving protection and is quick to get us to higher ground where we'll be safe. How reassuring it is to know that we can have strength, sustenance, and gentle grazing on the fertile grass that He finds for us in the midst of the storm! In fact, He always leads me to greener pastures where I can find rest for my soul.

It gives me great comfort to know that when I go through storms, He is right there with me. When we can look back upon where we've been, we discover that we have the strength to withstand the pressure as well as enjoy the beautiful fruit that glistens within the garden of our soul.

- **He Disciplines Us for Our Good**

Many times, the Lord disciplines us to refine us in order that we may become earthly reflections of His glory and others can see Him in us. But we may see it as punishment and misunderstand what He is doing in our lives. And if we grew up with a harsh disciplinary father, we might assume that God hovers over us with a big stick ready to pounce on our every mistake. Or, if we grew up with a dad who was absent due to work or travel, we may assume that God is also unavailable. As a result, we're unable to receive His never-failing love. The scriptures teach that He disciplines us for our good that we may share in His holiness. (See Hebrews 12:1)

- **He Gives Us Rest**

When we're weary and overwhelmed by worry and stress, the Shepherd allows us to be restored and replenished. He yokes Himself with us, which means He carries the burden, allowing us to find rest for our souls and even our bodies. During times when I wasn't sleeping well, I would meditate on Psalm 23 and trust that the Shepherd could bring me rest. It gives me great comfort to know that God will lead me into calm waters both emotionally and physically, where I can rest.

Accepting the Father's Love

Les: When Suzanne asked me to partner with her in writing some excerpts in the book, I found myself feeling reluctant. Some of the ideas that I have lived and will be sharing can be controversial based on the current popular party line of the religious community. I can now rest understanding that God is in charge and provides me with every positive feeling and sensation—the ones I used to believe only came from physical accomplishment (otherwise known as performance).

As I get older, I've found that when I accept the truth that everything happens for our good, my perception of events changes. In fact, I can see how the Lord has had His hand on my life from my earliest memories, which are surfacing more and more often as time goes by.

I think more memories expose themselves for two reasons. One is so I can return to the trauma and add the Spirit and the cleansing of tears that as a child I assumed meant I was weak and vulnerable. The other is to embrace that the Father's love has always been there no matter what circumstances I went through.

When I see life in a new way where the Lord is in charge, the world becomes a place full of wonder...a place where I can relate to the One who rules the world, a friend and Father who, when I ask anything in His name, will arrange my day so we can spend intimate time together.

I'd like to share some of the circumstances in my childhood where the Good Shepherd had His hands on me. My dad attended a Baptist Church pastored by his very religious aunt and uncle. I was stunned to discover that his uncle beat him all the time. It was hard to believe because my dad was a large man; at the age of seventeen, he was wearing men's size seventeen shirts. He told my mom that at age seventeen he needed to make a choice as to whether or not he would take the beatings anymore. In the end, he ran away from home to prevent the possibility of breaking his uncle in half.

Because of that negative religious background, my dad refused to allow his kids to have anything to do with religion. I remember my teenage sister putting religious figures on her windows with that spray-on stencil snow that was popular back then. He angrily told Mom to make her remove them.

I also knew he felt ill-equipped to raise children. One time when my oldest siblings were teenagers, Mom said to Dad that they needed to discuss how to handle problems with the kids. At that point, he said the kids were her responsibility, and he would provide the income. Mom said he was afraid he would be like his uncle and beat and possibly kill us, so he wanted nothing to do with parenting or discipline.

Later in life Mom told me that at that point she completely gave up and let us do what we wanted. Part of that is true, but if it was all true, I think we would have been much wilder and undisciplined than we were. Despite this, the Lord was taking care of me. When I was a child, I was very afraid of the dark and had to sleep with a nightlight. Sometimes I would wake in the night and be terrified. It came into my mind to read scripture. I began to keep a Bible wrapped in plastic under my pillow so I could get to it and read, though I had no idea what I was reading. As I read, I would get tired and relaxed. I then would put the Bible away and easily fall asleep. This habit began around the age of nine and continued until I was twelve.

At that point, I began to change for the worse, developing bad habits that included lying and shoplifting, although I was never caught. Though I was unaware of it, God already had His hand on me. When I was sixteen, my dad died. Three months before I turned eighteen, I was done with life and developed a plan to kill myself one night. However, the Lord had different ideas, and had me attend a church service that night where I met a friend and minister who served as my surrogate dad and introduced me to the Father. Immediately, my whole life changed. I quit stealing and lying and found a whole new reason to live. Later, as my eyes were opened, I was able to go back and apply the new truth to heal the early childhood traumas that had left me unable to believe in a loving father.

Soul Searching:

1. Describe the characteristics of your earthly father and how that has affected your relationship with Jesus or God the Father. Who do you struggle with in terms of receiving the love of Jesus or Father God?

2. Share a time when you were touched by the Father's love and gained more understanding of it. What did you learn that has greatly impacted you in your walk with Him?

3. Have you identified where you were in an overly dependent relationship and unable to experience healthy emotional connections with a partner or friend?

4. Do you have difficulty trusting that God is your Good Shepherd? In what areas listed above would you like to develop that trust relationship?

Chapter Three

Broken Cisterns

My people have done two evil things;
they have abandoned me, the spring of living water,
and have dug their own cisterns,
broken cisterns that cannot hold water.
—Jeremiah 2:13 (NIV)

W hy are we so blind and self-willed that we resort to doing things on our own? Why do we seek vices and clearly foolish paths that lead us to destruction? Just like sheep, we can be very stiff-necked individuals who think we know what is best. We seek pleasures that wet our whistle but tend to leave us empty and feeling like we're out on a limb alone. These enticements may give us momentary pleasure, but over time may cost us jobs, relationships, or even our health. Our pride and self-sufficiency kick in and tend to take over so that we become broken cisterns with very little room for a God who can restore our souls. This scripture in Jeremiah is a powerful visual image of what happens in people's lives. It's a picture of broken lives and barren souls longing for a way to fill those desperately empty places. In his book, *Abba's Child*, Author Brennan Manning says this: "When belonging to an elite group eclipses the love of God, when I draw life and meaning from any source other than my beloved, I am spiritually dead. When God gets relegated to second place behind any bauble or trinket, I have swapped the pearl of great price for painted fragments of glass."[4]

This quote is particularly relevant for those trying to create a relationship that will somehow satisfy every need. We long for that love need to be met, but somehow, we expect a partner or lover to fulfill that enormous empty vacuum. We forget that a partner is merely human, completely incapable of satisfying our deep inner needs. That's God's job!

Internal Blemishes

Unfortunately, we all carry into adulthood old internal wounds that cause us to make unhealthy connections that do nothing to meet our longing for love. We throw a tantrum trying to force that person to be what we need them to be, only to find that such behavior brings the end of the relationship. We live in a society that is quick to look for external objects to satisfy us, such as wealth, status, or power. We may seek a partner who can fill that need for status we're desperate to satisfy.

After sincere introspection, I have discovered that for most of my life I refused to believe that God sees me as valuable, even priceless, and sought my value from outward sources—especially performance. When we don't look to God to satisfy our needs, we resort to building up idols and becoming resentful when we fail to receive the true restoration that only He can give us.

Roles We Play

These days, people experience depressive episodes, anger and enraged outbursts, addictions, and emotional deadness that deeply affect their ability to make and maintain healthy connections. They may have had to fill a parental role, though they weren't properly nurtured themselves.

They may have been frightened when they witnessed their parents fighting, so they worried about being abandoned by their parents. Or they might have been forced to be a surrogate spouse to one of their parents and were not allowed to be children. For the most part, I see the lack of nurturing or affection from parents much like my own, who were distant or emotionally unavailable. Such family dynamics can have a huge negative impact on our emotional makeup, setting us up to make unhealthy connections. Psychologists have discovered a principle of attraction wherein we attract like magnets others who have the characteristics of our primary caretakers and then try to get from them what we lack. In other words, we often attract the very partner who is unable to give us the love we seek. We've all seen it—attraction to a wound-mate who has similar emotional hurts.

For a marriage to develop reciprocal emotional intimacy, the relationship must be made up of two emotionally healthy adults. For some not-so-healthy individuals, the point of making a whole out of two halves may be to find someone to complete them. They may also seek someone to meet an inner need that only God can fill. Through the years I have observed couples who wanted a healthy marriage comprised of one person playing the part of the mother and the other playing the part of the son or vice versa. The wounds they received and unnatural roles they played in childhood tend to prevent them from building healthy reciprocal adult partnerships. When one person is the adult, and the other person is the child in a relationship, there is little room for true intimacy to develop. If there has been sexual or emotional trauma in childhood, victims often seek the familiarity of those who reinforce the negative feelings of their early life. Those wounds can leave them enraged, and screaming to be understood, supported, and valued.

They may also build emotional walls to protect themselves from ever having to look inside. But those walls also block the Holy Spirit, preventing Him from ministering deep healing and peace. Walls can manifest in numerous behaviors including control of others, perfectionism, people pleasing and defensiveness. Just like Adam and Eve who felt the need to hide when they fell into sin, people can hide behind such behaviors and never discover the broken parts of their souls.

Sandra was raised by an alcoholic mom and a dad who clung to her as his surrogate spouse. She has childhood memories of going fishing and doing masculine things with dad, who looked to her as his activity buddy. She remembers feeling a great deal of shame about being a female whose sole purpose was to be used by men. Her mom's alcoholism left Sandra without the feminine connection for which she was so desperate.

She yearned to honor herself and have good boundaries with others, but she felt the only way to survive was to play the part of "tough girl." She gave up her God-given identity as the woman God had created her to be. She compensated by assuming a role as a fixer to please others, which left her even more frustrated, crying out for acceptance.

The marriage partner she attracted had qualities which were similar to those of her dad. He was quite wounded and tried to control her every move. He regularly put her down and humiliated her for her uniqueness, so that she grew quite depressed, having lost hope that she would ever feel worthy of being a woman, a wife or a businesswoman.

We identified generational strongholds of sexual patterns and beliefs she had formed that had led to much despair and resulted in an eating disorder. We used some Christ-centered energy releasing methods to free her from fears regarding sex and disempowerment from men. She found freedom from the food compulsion that had her hide food and consequently, rediscovered the real identity of the woman God had created her to be. I loved seeing how ready and willing she was to let the Holy Spirit do the work. Even though she had experienced tremendous pain growing up, God was able to repair her father image so she could begin to embrace the true Father she had so desperately desired.

What joy it is to see God do His work in this young woman's heart! Although not completely healed from pain, she has much more freedom to be her real self. Although she had previously spent years in counseling, she had never able to reach the level of freedom that the Lord accomplished in several months. Relationships tend to stir up our internal pain, which God can bring to light to address the cause and bring us to a place of peace.

> **Relationships tend to stir up our internal pain, which God can bring to light to address the cause and bring us to a place of peace.**

Deviating from the Path

When a shepherd doesn't lead his sheep with compassion and care, they may easily stray from safe pathways. They may venture into polluted, filthy ponds and be subject to all kinds of parasites and diseases that leave them sick and disabled. Perhaps they think the way we do, wondering, "What harm could come from straying from the path?" Just like sheep, the full impact of our stubborn, self-willed decisions begins to erode any chance of true emotional equilibrium or contentment.

Through the years I've seen the impact of such choices in my own life as well as in the lives of others. I've seen how my rebellious nature kicked in when I decided to do things my way.

There were times when I refused to wait on God's timing to bring the right partner into my life. I would date someone who wasn't the best fit just because I didn't want to feel alone. When I failed to listen to God's direction for my life I was subsequently led astray. After I saw that it didn't give me what I wanted, I was sheepishly led back to my Shepherd's path for me.

I often reflect on Isaiah 40:31:

"But those who wait on the LORD Shall renew *their* strength;

They shall mount up with wings like eagles;
They shall run and not be weary,
They shall walk and not faint."

Here God promises that if we wait on the Lord, He will supply the strength to rise above our circumstances. If we wait on Him, He will show us where we've gotten off track, and how we've believed lies that limit us in our marriages or life in general. It's important that we use patience during the process of self-examination rather than simply giving up or repeating the unhealthy choices of the past. If we are to be led by the Good Shepherd, we need to let Him guide us, which means we must yield our rights to have our way or run our own lives. If we allow the Spirit of God to direct us, we can trust Him to do a deep work in us as we make our way through challenging pastures. As we allow Christ to heal the broken cisterns we have hewn, they can be filled with the living water that brings joy and vitality to our lives. "He heals the brokenhearted and binds up their wounds." (Psalm 143:7)

Soul-Searching:

1. What area have you tried to fill with outward physical pursuits that left you void of fulfillment? Have you ever tried to get a spouse, partner or friend to fill up the emptiness inside you? What inner wounds did you try to get others to fill for you? i.e., shame, abandonment, unresolved grief, or resentments?

2. What roles have you played based on your established family patterns? What consequences did you face while

playing those roles? What protective behaviors have you acquired to hide behind? Perfectionism, people pleasing, control?

3. When have you been rebellious and sought to run your own life, failing to wait upon the Lord? What was the result? What can you do differently to help you wait upon the Lord to lead you into peaceful pastures?

Chapter Four

An Orphan's Journey

My father and my mother abandoned me. I'm like an
orphan! But you took me in and made me yours.
—Psalm 27:10 (TPT)

I f you still doubt that Christ will be there to meet you where
you are, keep reading. The testimony of my dear friend
Sasha has so deeply touched me that I have devoted an
entire chapter to the way she's embraced the Father's loving
commitment amid tremendous struggles.

Sasha was conceived out of wedlock, to seventeen-year-old
parents who divorced two years later. She has no memory of
living with her father. When she was two years old, her whole

world was turned upside down, and she lost her ability to laugh or find enjoyment in anything, including food. The family doctor diagnosed her with depression due to the divorce and the drastic changes that left her feeling insecure. When her mother took a job to support the two of them, she had to put Sasha in daycare. With an emotionally absent mother and an unavailable father, her world no longer seemed safe and happy. Sasha remembers very little of her childhood.

Soon her mother remarried, and it wasn't long until eight-year-old Sasha became the caretaker of two younger siblings—a six-month-old and a one-year-old toddler! She felt abandoned, terribly unhappy, unloved and frustrated with responsibilities far beyond her abilities. Her parents took advantage of her, using her as a constant babysitter and leaving her feeling desperate for love. And because she grew up with no supervision, she struggled to distinguish right from wrong.

Sasha felt increasingly uncomfortable around her mother's new husband while living in a household deeply impacted by both alcoholism and constant loud arguments. When she was only seven, her stepfather used a knife to threaten her mom, who screamed at Sasha to call the police. The responsibility for the two brothers laid heavily on her young shoulders. At the age of eleven, she was molested by her stepfather. So, during nights when her mother wasn't home, she began hiding in the closet so her stepfather couldn't find her. She lived in constant fear and anxiety, never feeling safe or secure, and because she had no one to protect her, she learned never to trust anyone.

Looking back, Sasha says she felt like she never had a childhood. She rarely had freedom to relax or play as a child. Because of her past, she developed relationships with men who were emotionally unavailable, dishonest or unstable. As a result, Sasha succumbed to an abortion at age fifteen. The ensuing guilt from the abortion led her to thoughts of suicide, and that guilt has haunted her ever since. At age fifteen she was still living at home, serving as the primary caretaker for her younger brothers. Feeling empty and lost, she used drugs to medicate the pain. Unlike other drug users of that day, she didn't have to hide her drug use from her mother because they took them together. Drugs were Sasha's escape from reality, and she experimented with whatever she could get her hands on, including heroin. Cocaine became her drug of choice.

We often picture drug users as dirty and living on the streets, but Sasha was an exception to that image. At age twenty, she was a model whose photos appeared on magazine covers. She was driving an expensive sports car and living next door to multi-millionaires. Although she looked like the picture of happiness, broken dreams come in a wide variety of deceptively glitzy packages. The truth is that beneath the glamour and glitz, Sasha was extremely unhappy.

Her life took an even more destructive turn in Aspen, Colorado, a place she called "the Hollywood of the mountains." There, Sasha found herself living the high life that offered anything she could ever want. She was enamored by the fast pace and upscale drug parties, moving in circles with movie stars. She felt sophisticated attending ballets and plays, listening to classical music while snorting cocaine off a silver platter.

In her circles, everyone referred to the way it always snowed in Aspen, but they didn't mean frozen rain—they meant cocaine, which was readily available.

Before arriving in Aspen, Sasha went to a church where they offered an altar call, which only confused her. To her surprise, it wasn't what she anticipated. It was a big church with a large congregation. The members were singing positive, upbeat songs accompanied by a band, and they seemed to have some things that she sorely lacked: peace, joy, and happiness.

As she left the church that day, a man stopped her and asked how long she'd been attending. She replied that it was her first visit. When he asked if she was saved, she burst into tears and said she didn't know what that meant. He asked if she would like to know what it meant. She said "yes". Right there in that parking lot on a warm summer day, she asked Jesus into her heart. Deep inside, she had always believed there had to be a higher power and more to life. She didn't realize until much later that this was the most important decision she would ever make in her life. Eight years later it would be critical that she had said the salvation prayer.

Fast forward to New Year's Eve in Aspen, when most of the movie stars were in town. A group of Sasha's friends were ready to party with more than two pounds of cocaine. Four days later they were still partying with no sleep or food—only cocaine and alcohol. At that point, Sasha was feeling delirious. She knew that she couldn't keep going without sleep. She went home and was so high that her heart felt like it was beating out of her chest. She was wondering what she could do to come down when she remembered that she had a bottle of Valium prescribed by her doctor. Desperate to sleep, she wasn't in a good frame of mind and wasn't thinking rationally when she opened the bottle and dumped a handful of Valium pills into her hand. She only vaguely remembered that her girlfriend called and didn't like the way she sounded. Sasha admitted that she might have taken too many pills. Fortunately for Sasha, her girlfriend arrived, found her unresponsive, and called for help just in the nick of time. Of course, Sasha has no recollection of that event because she was hovering precariously between life and death.

The next thing Sasha knew, she was heading toward an incredible light where there was no fear, only peace. As she got closer to the light, there was a faint but visible image of a man she recognized—the Son of God. She couldn't describe His features because He was full of light. But she felt immersed in the most incredible love that words could not convey. It was an undefiled, pure and holy love that she had never encountered anywhere else. They communicated without spoken words, and He asked why she was doing drugs. Without hesitation, she replied, "I'm unhappy."

> Sasha was heading toward an incredible light where there was no fear, only peace.

Behind Him, she could see the most gorgeous scenery, far more beautiful than anything on earth. It was so magnificent that it completely captured her attention. He said that if she walked through the door behind Him, she would leave life as she knew it. After a moment's thought, she said that she didn't want to leave, she just wanted to be happy. Then He said, "If you follow me, you'll be happy." She said "ok".

Suddenly, Sasha was awakened in the emergency room where a doctor was trying to revive her. When she was in this other dimension, she felt very much alive. She had no other thoughts—only that she experienced an incredibly beautiful light. When she was back in her body in the emergency room, she heard a nurse tell the doctor that she had no vital signs as they continued to work on reviving her. When the doctor came into her room the next morning, he informed her that they'd almost lost her the previous night.

That experience changed Sasha's life forever. She's convinced that she met the Lord at the gates of heaven, and if she had walked through the door, she would have died in the emergency room at 28 years of age. That's why it was so important that she said the salvation prayer in the parking lot of the church eight years earlier. She is certain that had she not accepted the Lord's gift of salvation she would be dead, and the destiny of her soul would now be in question.

Sasha was addicted to drugs for sixteen years when not a single day passed without them. She never had peace, but she didn't know any better—it was just a way of life. On the outside, it appeared that she was living a perfect life. She had no clue what it was to love or feel true happiness. But she took Emmanuel's (meaning: God with us) advice and decided to follow Him. The scripture that stands out to her is John 8:12, "I am the light of the world. He who follows me shall not walk in darkness but have the light of life."

Now, decades later Sasha is happy and at peace. She hasn't taken any drugs since that experience. Of course, she still deals with the same struggles which we all face while we're alive. But somehow, the peace and love she felt that night is still present. She says she will never forget the night when she was drawn toward an incredible light, immersed in God's endless love. That night she found the one true Savior, whose love never fails, and whose word never returns void. According to Psalm 68:5, Jesus is a Father to the fatherless, adopting us into His family. Through the years, Sasha has become very passionate about Him and calls Him "Abba Father"—the Hebrew name for Daddy.

Her experience and conversation with Jesus left an impressionable, non-wavering imprint in her heart. She was determined to find out more about having a relationship with the Son of God. Through the gracious love of a pastor and his wife, she was able to go through agonizing weeks of detoxing along with months of counseling to deal with childhood pain. Sasha looks back over her life and realizes that there's no way under that she could have changed her life on her own, under her own strength. When she stopped taking drugs, she lost all the people who she thought were her close friends. At that point in life, she had one person to turn to—the one who came to set the captives free, to whom she is eternally grateful.

Sasha has truly seen and experienced God as a True Father to her little orphan heart. She is convinced that she is deeply loved and that He has sustained her ever since the day she nearly died. She has been a tremendous testimony to me of the redemptive power of the Father's love. I am encouraged by Sasha's courage to share her story. I know her desire is that others will find freedom from whatever bondage they are going through. They can also, then, experience the love of God that heals the broken-hearted.

Soul-Searching:

1. Take a moment to reflect on Sasha's powerful story. What emotions did her story evoke in you?

2. What father or mother wounds have you felt from your parents that have impacted you? In what ways has the wounding affected your life in terms of your relationships and co-workers?

3. Are there addictive behaviors that you formed as an escape, or coping strategies that you devised to cover up feeling orphaned and abandoned?

Chapter Five
Making Friends with Feelings

Search me, O God, and know my heart; Try me and
know my anxieties; And see if there be any wicked way
in me, And lead me in the way everlasting.
—Psalm 139:23-24 (NKJV)

Our negative feelings and turmoil are barometers of the pain we carry. They lead us to the source of the wounds that prevent us from living life abundantly, with nothing missing or broken. Just like Adam and Eve hid once they fell into sin, we tend to hide our shame and refuse to look at the underlying issues that influence our emotions because they're too uncomfortable. As children, our families tend to have "no feel" rules. When little Janie has feelings, she is told not to be so sensitive and just put on a happy face. This forces Janie to deny and ignore her very nature. As children, we're filled with feelings and need to feel safe enough to express them.

This situation is much like the one I encountered as a child. My mother was very uncomfortable with her feelings, always telling me to pull myself together and get over them. Sadly, she grew up to be a very stoic, shut-down woman in her later years because she had made a habit of suppressing whatever feelings she had.

When children learn early on to stuff feelings, they grow up as adults who are shut off from their emotions, which can eventually lead to emotional numbness. Typically, the root of such numbness is a feeling of unworthiness. Dr. Brené Brown, who has done a great deal of research, shares in her book *Daring Greatly*: "We numb the pain that comes from feeling inadequate and 'less than.' But that was only part of the puzzle. Anxiety and disconnection also emerged as drivers of numbing in addition to shame. The most powerful need for numbing seems to come from combinations of all three—shame, anxiety, and disconnection."[5]

Anxiety can arise when life feels out of control because our feelings have gotten too big and unmanageable to contain. Life experiences bring out all sorts of emotions that typically get denied. We tend to become disconnected from others, ourselves, and most of all from God. Our lack of connection with ourselves results in living out of a false self to mask any tinge of vulnerability. We develop roles such as the "good girl" or the "tough guy" to camouflage our inner selves when we feel unequal to a task or face situations beyond our control.

> Anxiety can arise when life feels out of control because our feelings have gotten too big and unmanageable to contain.

The good news is that our Good Shepherd can step in to be that comfort zone with open-armed support to walk us through any disconnection with our emotions. He can be the one to solely connect with us so we can be truly vulnerable to share whatever is on our heart. I believe the psalmist David experienced the same type of openness when his honesty brought him to his knees. He continually released his emotional agonies to God. His feelings were clearly raw and despairing when he admitted his deep heartache to the Lord. In fact, this seemed to bring him to a place of deeper connection to the very heart of God.

There were times as a child when my emotions grew so intense that I didn't know what to do with them. It started early in my childhood when I had crying spells that left my mother wondering what to do with me. I often used temper tantrums, trying desperately to keep them going long and loud enough that my parents would come to my rescue. And when that didn't happen, I was left to deal with my uncontrollable feelings on my own with no one to comfort me. Fortunately, once I released many of those feelings, I felt better. Children usually have an advantage because they deal with emotions by instantly releasing them, which enables them to be off and running again. Adults don't do this very well because they've learned to keep a tight lid on their emotions and not allow them to surface freely. Over time,

I have found that when people allow themselves to embrace their emotions, they no longer need to hold onto them. I like to think of emotions as energy in motion trying to move through the body, which makes discharging them the natural release that God designed.

Many people are terrified when confronted by their painful feelings. They may think they will get stuck there and not be able to move through them to a place of resolution. In fact, when we were first married, my husband Les, who had a great deal of childhood pain, would suddenly burst out crying. As you can imagine, this behavior didn't fit with my idea of the mature, masculine man I married, and it left me fearful that he wouldn't be able to resolve his feelings. Having never dealt with such things before, I was surprised that, with the help of the Holy Spirit, he successfully moved on to resolution. Later, I could see that he experienced the fruit of that process. Below he shares openly one of the critical memories for which he received healing.

God the Pursuer

Les: I can always count on God to pursue me, to clean up all residual self-hatred. This hatred developed whenever I did something shameful in my early years. One event, in particular, left me feeling ashamed and unworthy, unable to forgive myself for something I had completely forgotten.

I find it incredible to realize that God gently works to expose memories that I don't know are hidden deep within me. One day, about twelve years ago, my left arm and shoulder began to cause me increasing pain. I did the usual things to relieve it, moving it around, rubbing it, but nothing helped. In fact, the pain grew more intense.

Then, it occurred to me that I should allow the pain to build, and not resist it. As the pain increased, I felt I was to let it take me where it needed to go. In the process, a memory surfaced of a very abusive incident that occurred when I was seven years old. My mom's boyfriend was lying in wait in our root cellar to take advantage of my innocence and abuse me sexually. Another time I was twenty minutes late getting home, and when I arrived, he was livid that I had made him wait. My dad's rifle was standing against a post beside him. I was terrified when he took the rifle and said, "This is what happens when you're late." He took the rifle and shot my cat, who was curled up in the corner.

I ran over to the cat, picked it up and tried to cradle it in my arms. In complete panic, it tried to get out of my arms and scratched me as it died. Then the man said, "Take the cat, throw it in the trash outside, and get back in here." When I came back, I noticed a knife on the shelf. I grabbed it and tried to stab him in the stomach. He caught my hand before I could stab him and wrenched my arm behind my back. It was the Lord's timing to bring back the memory that clearly explained why my arm and shoulder were hurting.

I don't remember what happened after that. I figured my mom found out about the incident and got rid of him. When that memory surfaced, the gate opened, and the tears just flowed unchecked, accompanied by other lost memories. As the Lord took me back to other memories of abuse, I realized that my mom's boyfriend abused me twice before the incident with the cat. I had to keep returning to the memories and let the tears flow to cleanse and relieve the hurt. I believe the scripture that says: "Prayers (conversations) sowed in tears with the Lord shall be reaped in joy." (Psalm 126:5) This passage always gives me hope that releasing the pent-up emotions will allow my heart to heal.

As a small boy, I wanted to learn to catch a baseball, but my brothers didn't have time to teach me. My mom's boyfriend said he would teach me if I let him do things to me. He abused me several times before I argued that he hadn't kept his promise to teach me how to catch a baseball. I had to keep returning to those memories until I could fully release the pain entirely. I was particularly upset that I had permitted him to hurt me, and that made me hate myself. I felt that I had brought it all on myself, even the death of my cat. After all the memories had surfaced, I was finally able to release the lie that I was responsible, when I'd been an innocent seven-year-old. When I could recall that memory and grieve over it and finally let it go, the pain in my arm and shoulder disappeared! I now feel confident that even burdens I have yet to face can be released when the timing is right and when the Lord is in it.

Jesus Encounters

Suzanne: When I have walked people through intense feelings from their childhoods, Jesus often shows up in the memory, showing them that He was there for them even during the traumatic event. He never left them. If only I had known "the Comforter" when I was a child, it would have allowed me to receive His loving touch during the traumatic events I faced. I'm always comforted by the passage found in Hebrews 4:15: "For we do not have a High Priest who cannot sympathize with our weak-nesses but was in all points tempted as we are, yet without sin. Let us, therefore, come boldly unto the throne of grace, that we may obtain mercy and find grace to help in time of need."

Christ is aware of the emotions we face and can identify with every one of them because as a man He felt them all! What a great comfort to know He designed us to have emo-tions—in fact, He designed them all. So why do so many of us walk around feeling that we need to squelch them? Why do we think we aren't walking in sync with God if we have negative feelings? Our subconscious works hard to catalog away all of our life experiences so that we never, ever have to feel them. As a result, they can become deeply buried until something triggers them to surface and show their ugly heads. I like to think of this as a comfort zone that we have lived with that will do whatever it takes to maintain its hold on us. For years we may have learned to resist our painful feelings, so it becomes a familiar place to reside. A popular book I often refer to is: *Feel-ings Buried Alive Never Die* by Karol Truman, who describes how such intense feelings never leave until we can feel and release them.[6]

Now, I see my emotional makeup from a new point of view: When I experience strong feelings, I need to pay atten-tion; God is saying I'm holding onto something that hinders me from receiving His freedom and peace. Either past trauma triggers me, or I have a yearning for something that the world can't satisfy. It may be something that I anticipate will make me feel valued, like being successful, a good author, or having the approval of others.

Many of the emotions we deal with can be traced back to beliefs or vows. If we believe that feelings are unacceptable and vow to suppress them, we'll struggle for permission to engage in them fully, because we won't violate a vow we've made. We may find ourselves involved in addictive behavior to suppress our feelings. My addiction wasn't beer or ice cream binges, but rather busyness, worry, love obsession, or working incessantly to avoid and numb my feelings.

I have a picture in my bedroom that depicts Christ holding a little lamb. It comforts me to be reminded that I just need to come to Him and let Him hold me in my pain. I need to see that nothing is too emotionally enormous for Him to walk me through. When I observe those who want to take their lives, I'm aware of how intense emotions can become when they're suppressed. They know no other escape, except to numb out entirely by making their final exit. It saddens me to see them refuse to reach out to God, the Good Shepherd who has solutions to every problem.

Recently a woman came in to see me. She had an immense number of emotions and was primarily unable to address the issues in her marriage. She had been a "giver" her entire life, to the point where she ignored her own personal needs. She had given physically and financially to her three kids and her extended family, giving them whatever they needed. She gave herself continually to satisfy her husband's needs, but somehow, it had never been enough to make him love her. She told me she had everything she longed for monetarily but felt lonely and discontented in her marriage.

She spent much of the session weeping. I said I would ask the Lord to help her, and as I prayed, the Lord directed me to take her back to the little girl inside her and invite Jesus into the scene. There she embraced the love of the Father in a way that can only come from the heart of Jesus. He showed her He was with her all along—that He loved her and would always accept her even though her path had led her to destructive behavior in her past. He showed her that with His help, she could overcome any difficulty and that she no longer needed to subvert her own needs in favor of the needs of others to earn their love. As tears continued to stream down her cheeks, I saw Jesus come in and shower love into the heart of that precious little girl. It was a magnificent sight to see!

Moving Through Feelings

I like to encourage people to make friends with their feelings. Like a television set, you have a current running through your body. If you tampered with the electrical system of your television by poking around, it wouldn't give you a clear picture. Just like our television sets, when we create negative emotions through our thought patterns, the flow of good energy is disrupted. You might first start with where you are feeling it in your body. It might show up in a stomachache or pain in your arm such as Les experienced.

What if you don't know what you are feeling? I hear this from many. Some people don't even have a vocabulary for their feelings. The difficulty can be the inability to identify what feelings you are experiencing. I learned a great tool called a sentence stem from Nathaniel Branden, who is a psychologist and author of many books on the topic.[7] You start out with a sentence stem such as: "I am angry because." You then brainstorm everything you are feeling to complete that sentence eight times. This exercise will pull out of yourself a theme regarding what you are really feeling. It's a great way to identify what you are unaware of in your inner terrain.

This is another exercise I like. Imagine yourself cutting through "the story" or perception you made up about what happened and just move through the feelings that lie underneath. Many times, the story is only your perception of what happened. If you eliminate the story and allow yourself to feel the emotions that accompany the experience, you can release them, feel them and allow them to dissipate. It's not something to fear or avoid. Suppressing those feelings prevents the Good Shepherd from doing His work within us, which then allows the energy to become stagnant inside our cells. It's those emotions that can eventually create painful behaviors or communication blocks within our relationships. Once we allow ourselves to feel the emotions, we can identify the thinking that caused the emotion and take it to the Lord so that He can touch and heal the deep wounds inside us.

Soul-Searching:

1. Are your choices and activities comforting and nourishing your spirit or are they ways to avoid difficult emotions? Are you comfortable moving into your negative feelings when they surface, or do you try to suppress them and push them away?

2. Can you identify a negative feeling such as pain, fear or anger that manifested in physical symptoms? What story did you make up that might have created the negative

emotion? How could you start to make friends with this feeling and let go of that story or perception?

3. What were the messages you heard in your upbringing about feelings? Was it okay to express negative feelings or did your family have "no-feel rules" that taught you to suppress them?

4. How can embracing our feelings and create more intimacy in our relationships with God and others? Do we share with our partner or friends what we are feeling, or do we hide behind the "good Christian façade" and deflect from our emotions?

5. Have you ever had a Jesus encounter where He met you in your pain from a difficult situation or memory? Share with others what you experienced.

Transformation Prayer

Heavenly Father, search my heart and help me discover what I'm feeling. Allow me to feel in my body where I have held onto this emotion. Give me the courage to move into the very center of this feeling and release whatever thought or perception keeps me from feeling the emotion. Allow me to fully feel the emotion, getting to the very core of it, so it can grow smaller and begin to dissipate. Reveal the origins of the faulty beliefs that have brought about this feeling. Show me what these beliefs are so I can fully release them. Reveal your truth as I allow every aspect of my spirit, soul, and body to come into harmony with my identity in Christ.

Chapter Six

Salvation as a Daily Walk

*The spirit of the Son is in us and is always
leading us to the Father. So you must choose
what and who will lead your life. If you
say yes to the Spirit, you yield to the life
of Jesus that is being formed in you.*
—Neil Lozano

The Greek word "*sozo*" means "to be saved." Strong's Concordance defines it as: saved, healed, delivered, protected, preserved, and to be made whole (in spirit, soul, and body). I believe salvation is a daily experience of taking our feelings to the Lord—doubts, fears, and anxious thoughts that weigh us down so we can be delivered from them and experience abundant life in Christ.

As lost sheep, we're weak and broken and need to feed on the comforting power that the Good Shepherd makes available to us every day. By taking our feelings to Him, He can begin working with them to restore the spiritual fruit for which we long. Philippians 2:12-13 says to "work out your own salvation with fear and trembling. For it is God who works in you both to will and do for His good pleasure." We aren't to walk in fear, but rather with great reverence; we're to trust that He is stirring up things in our souls to bring about healing and a closer relationship with Him. Just like any human relationship, it requires listening, talking to Him, and taking our concerns to Him daily. Then He takes every thought that creates pain and exchanges it for the peace that is beyond all understanding. (Philippians 4:7)

> **Just like any human relationship, it requires listening, talking to Him, and taking our concerns to Him daily.**

I've asked Les to share some of his thoughts about how he has been able to apply the "working out of his salvation" daily. I marvel at the way he has developed a wonderful, intimate relationship with the Lord and how He has met him in his greatest need.

Les: One of the best parts of relating to Christ inside of me is that He is always there—and boy, do I need Him! Once I understood that Christ is within me, every second of every day, I now look for the connection with Him, and He uses my circumstances to bring me closer.

I want to clarify that this realization has not matured overnight. The Lord revealed himself to me when I was about to turn eighteen because I was done with life. I had planned to kill myself that very night. From age eighteen to twenty-eight, I only understood scripture to be laws I had to obey but could not live out. During that time, I was terrified of my feelings because they contradicted "who I was supposed to be" according to my understanding of scripture. As a result, I was very judgmental and condemning toward myself and others.

As the years went by, I learned to become a friend to my feelings. Being a friend has allowed a wonder-filled journey, discovering who I am and who I was meant to be...the one Christ has already accepted and loves. When I finally understood and accepted the truth that He's in control of everything, I had someone to whom I could express my negative feelings about what was happening in my life. He's not only a source of power but a friend who can answer my prayers—prayers that continually develop our relationship. I'm still puzzled to know that He listens to whatever complaint or lament I have, allowing me to recognize my real self—my helpless, sinful self.

He is delighted when I stand in a checkout line feeling impatient and in need of His presence. I don't like feeling impatient, so because I know He's the author of patience, I ask Him to give it to me. Through faith, I know He can give me the fruits of the spirit if I confess that I need them.

In another instance, I was left doing the dishes one evening when my wife headed for the bedroom. For the most part, she cooks, and I do the dishes. But one night, I felt burdened by the vast number of dishes piled before me, and I was upset that she had used so many to make dinner, which was delicious and satisfying, so that wasn't the problem. To be honest, my anger was increasing by the second, wishing she would come and help me. I told the Lord I hated doing dishes and my next thought was: "If she comes out and helps you, what will that accomplish?" Then it occurred to me, "Don't you just want to lose the anger about doing the dishes?" Of course, in my mind, having her do part of them was the same thing and I told the Lord so. Then it dawned on me that I would be fine if I could just feel patience. Call it a miracle or whatever you want, but I suddenly felt patience. I was so overwhelmed by the thought that the Lord was taking care of me in my distress... that I whistled through the rest of the dishes.

From what I understand, this is what the relationship is all about. It's taking part in what's available on the other side...the love, joy, patience, and longsuffering that we want to experience every day. I'm not that familiar with Hebrew, but I understand that the true meaning of the name Hebrew is, "people of the other side." The other side is the spiritual side of life: Christ giving me the fruits of the spirit in each circumstance when I humble myself enough to ask.

Suzanne: Les' example shows that rather than being afraid of the Lord and becoming distant, we need to know that God is always there for us at the moment. David knew this very well when He said, "God is our refuge and strength, a very present help in trouble." (Psalm 46:1) If we go to Him with our feelings, He's quick to offer whatever we need at any given moment. "But the fruit of the Spirit is love, joy, peace, longsuffering, kindness, goodness, faithfulness, gentleness, self-control. Against such things, there is no law." (Galatians 5:22)

Years ago, I worked with Campus Crusade for Christ, explaining the plan of salvation using the *Four Spiritual Laws* outreach booklet. We shared the scripture, "But as many as received Him, to them He gave the right to become children of God, to those who believe in His name." (John 1:12) In the Greek, the word "receive" is defined as "taking hold of and bringing into yourself." I don't think this means we're supposed to receive Christ into our hearts and then passively wait for Him to toss blessings to us, hoping we'll mature. Rather we are to take an active role, daily working out our struggles as He leads the way.

During those years, we also shared a booklet that explained that in order to walk in the Spirit we must fully surrender to Him as Lord of our lives, releasing to Him any negative feelings that rob us of our peace. Only then can He give us whatever we need. We just need to trust that He is available to meet us wherever we are so we can experience the intimacy that the Good Shepherd offers us at the moment.

Soul-Searching:

1. Are you focused on what you want God to do outwardly instead of what He can do in your spirit? How does this translate into your everyday life?

2. Can you see how working out your salvation is a daily experience? Can you truly bring all your feelings to the Lord, no matter how insignificant? Give an example of how you might incorporate this into your daily relationship with Him.

3. Do you allow yourself to daily surrender your pain to the Lord? If so, what fruits have you found available to you as you fully surrender?

Chapter Seven

Are You Ready and Willing?

If you have the courage to allow Him into every room
of your life, He will come in and redecorate every room,
so it is more beautiful than you ever imagined possible.
But you never know until you start opening those doors.
—Katherine Walden

Y ou might have heard the following saying: "When the student is ready, the teacher appears." I like to think of this in spiritual terms. When we're ready and willing, the Good Shepherd appears and begins to pursue us to bring healing and restoration to our soul and body. Many times, a memory surfaces that we had no idea would be there. The Lord is ready to apply His healing balm to that memory, but it's up to us to be ready and willing to bring it to Him.

I often ask people this question: "Are you willing to receive healing?" Jesus passed over many people whom He discerned were not willing. He asked the invalid who had been disabled for thirty-eight years: "Do you want to get well?" (John 5:6 NIV) In this verse the word "well" is the Greek word *hugios* that translates as "whole." I believe He was asking if he wanted to experience wholeness in spirit, soul, and body here on earth.

There are people who perpetually search for the right therapist who can rescue them, so their emotional problems will disappear as if by magic. Often it seems there is a payoff or reward for repeating a familiar pattern however counterproductive, as evidenced by their refusal to take responsibility. This resistance can be deeply buried in the subconscious and show up in emotions they refuse to relinquish.

I like to think of it as a familiar shoe. It fits and is very comfortable since it's broken in, but it doesn't wear well over time. Many times, holding onto damaged emotions fulfills some perceived need to feel safe or not let an abuser off the hook. For example, we may think that if we distance ourselves from others, it will protect us from hurt, rejection or even abandonment. But the reality is that we need to overcome such resistance to retrieve what we are repressing. This is called "secondary gain" because there is some perceived benefit to staying where we are instead of making changes.

It's paramount that we let go of what we've held onto in order to open up and allow ourselves to move forward effectively. And though it goes against everything we believe it does set us free.

There is an obstruction toward change that occurs when there's a disconnection between the two planes—the belief systems of the conscious and unconscious minds. It may manifest as unanswered prayer, scriptures that fail to transform our thinking, repeating the same unwanted behavior, and affirmations that mean nothing. James 1:8 calls this scenario double-mindedness. "He is a double-minded man, unstable in all his ways." When the left and right hemispheres of the brain that contain both the thinking/conscious mind and the feeling/subconscious mind are not in agreement, it's nearly impossible to have a healthy, integrated mind. And because there is disagreement between those two hemispheres, we can't experience the wholeness God designed for us to live out. It's only when both sides are in single-minded agreement that we live in peaceful harmony with ourselves, others and God, with nothing missing or broken and we experience a sense of well-being that can't be found elsewhere.

> There is an obstruction toward change that occurs when there's a disconnection between the conscious and unconscious minds.

One way to identify double-mindedness is to write out an affirmation. Notice whether you have trouble believing it. What thoughts arise that contradict what you've written down? That will quickly help you identify what you really believe and what you need to do to clear the obstruction before you can accept the affirmation as truth.

I may believe in my thinking mind that I'm His beloved and worthy of receiving love from God, but my subconscious feeling brain may be programmed with thoughts of shame due to memories from my past. This disconnect brings frustration because we may know what the scripture says, but for some reason, those verses haven't yet come alive to set us free. The subconscious can control as much as 90% of what we believe and how we behave consequently.

Freedom through Healing Methods

In my early years of practice, I practiced Theophostic ministry (now called Transformation Prayer Ministry, developed by Dr. Edward Smith) to set people free from their pain.[8] I would invite Jesus to be there with them in the memory, allowing the Holy Spirit to help them clear out the rooted negative belief. In the process, they would be able to hear His truth, replacing the lies they believed. But I discovered that if people have little or no capacity to receive the Father's love, they will struggle to resolve the issue successfully. Or, if they failed to receive the ongoing love of their parents early on, they may not be able to hear Jesus' voice when He speaks in the traumatic memory. Being able to build up a capacity to receive the Father's love is critical to embrace before going into painful memories.

More recently, I have worked with a Christ-centered method called Splankna Therapy that is a mind/body approach and has proven highly effective with some clients. In her book *Splankna: The Redemption of Energy Healing for the Kingdom of God*, Author Sarah J. Thiessen explains a protocol for clearing out the negative cellular memories of past events, ultimately helping people find redemption and healing.[9] By allowing the truth to penetrate and saturate the wrong beliefs encoded in the cellular memory, the body's hard drive is defragmented, giving people a chance to heal.

The Splankna method can clear out generational strong-holds, themes that affect victims over a lifetime, as well as those affecting specific age periods. We are able to access certain emotional data, and it is cleared out through a focused inten-tion along with a prayer of repentance that releases the enemy's legal rights to an area.

I used this method with Kathy, who came to me for help regarding sexual intimacy with her husband. She had already invested a great deal of time and money in therapy doing guided prayer ministry and behavioral work to bring healing in that area. Unfortunately, none of those practices produced the break-through she sought. She understood that her history of trauma and sexual abuse affected her love life, but she had no idea how to access healing.

Initially, it was her daughter's angry outburst toward her as well as her own difficulty falling asleep that caused her to seek further help. She said her responses are often triggered by the anger of others and that she tends to withdraw when she feels unsafe. She hadn't had sex with her husband in years. She came from a non-religious background but was fortunate to come to know Jesus at a young age. She and her husband are both com-mitted believers who have been in therapy for other issues. My heart goes out to the many couples who struggle in this area; in fact, it's a common problem today. But the truth is that in these cases, a deeper root from the past is usually in operation.

As we began working together, the first area that the Lord began working on with Kathy was a tremendous self-hatred that was masked by a need to perform to feel valued. She identified with the lie that says, "I'm not valuable if I'm not needed, so I need to perform perfectly." She went to great lengths to be perfect enough to be accepted. Several weeks into our sessions she said she no longer felt the need to drive herself. We rejoiced that the first layer of healing had begun to shape her identity in Christ.

After a releasing session with me, I assigned homework that allowed her to retrain her mind, saturating herself in new beliefs to replace the lies she had embraced. It wasn't long before the next layer of issues revealed itself: her much older brother had molested her years earlier. After he repeatedly peeped in her bedroom window or fondled her in her sleep, she had been conditioned to dread going to sleep. Negative emotions were cleared out of the anguish, dread, and shame she had previously been unable to acknowledge.

We identified a generational stronghold that had come through her dad's side of the family, a pattern of dissociation where she had split off a part of her soul to carry the trauma. I explained that this form of dissociation occurs when there is too much pain for a young child to deal with at the time. In our efforts to compartmentalize the pain we seal it up in a closet, so we never have to deal with it again. After working through the pain, Kathy no longer had an adrenaline rush that kept her awake when she tried to fall asleep, nor did she need to be on high alert. In fact, she was amazed that she now felt able to make love with her husband on a daily basis—a quick turnaround to say the least! When she included her husband during one of our sessions, he confirmed that she was no longer as perfectionistic and that their sexual intimacy had returned. I was very encouraged to see what God had done in her marriage and life!

Buried Emotions

This woman's story is a vivid example of how our buried emotions from the past can show up in unwanted behavior in the here and now. Marital counseling typically focuses on trying to make behavioral changes. But no matter how much we try to change, if the emotions are deeply rooted in our hearts, they may still wreak havoc in our lives until they are removed entirely. The telltale sign is that while we use every available help to inspire change, we still struggle in an ongoing losing battle.

Just as it happened in Kathy's case, if we allow the Lord to help us take ownership of the emotion and trace it back to its roots, it stands a far greater chance of being cleared and disarmed, losing its power over us. Once we identify and own the issue, the original root can be plucked out, so that we are automatically transformed at heart. When this happens, the Lord can then share His truth to counteract whatever lies were driving those feelings.

Beliefs that are rooted in childhood tend to be irrational and fear-based because children feel responsible for what happens in their environment. The first six years of a child's life are critical since the events of those years tend to be directly hardwired into the brain. Thus, the beliefs formed in those years cause an adult to mistakenly interpret what happens later in life. Even emotions that the child felt in the womb can continue to affect that person as an adult. Clients often report that as children, they felt their problems were their own fault. Some said, "I'm all alone—no one is there for me." "I'm unlovable." "I must be bad since my mom and dad divorced." Though their beliefs are completely irrational, they tend to be deeply implanted in the adult's present-day thinking, and deeply impact their day-to-day outlook.

Our Good Shepherd is committed to not let us remain stuck in our emotional lies. We need to trust that it is *His job to set us free*. As much as we want to fix our brokenness, receiving the Father's love will set us free to heal as we follow where He leads us. Our role is to embrace the Father, focus on Him, and identify and relinquish our hold on whatever keeps us in bondage. We must let go of the need to do it in our strength and choose to believe that He will do the "good work" within us.

In the past, I tended to view what God was doing as punitive. How could a loving God dredge up painful issues especially in marriages that seem so impossible to redeem? Since that time, I've come to understand that the pain is inside me and it's only because of His compassion that He dredges it up to heal it. He wants me to embrace the completeness of His finished work in my life, so that I can live out my destiny, completely unhindered. I just need to be patient with the process. The emotional wounds that I hold onto are in the way of walking out His plan for my life.

The Good Shepherd is waiting for us to take these strongholds to Him, so He can free us to soar as never before! He loves us so much that He wants us to be released, set free from emotions that enslaved us as innocent victims. Then He can make beauty out of our ashes!

Soul-Searching:

1. Are you aware that you could be resisting God's best plan, refusing to address areas that feel too comfortable to release, i.e., your marriage, your addiction, depression or anxiety? Can you identify benefits or a perceived gain from staying where you are? What has it cost you?

2. Has your partner tripped your emotional trigger, so that you blamed him or her? Try to identify the lies you believe that might be rooted in your childhood.

3. Identify one reason you might be double-minded because of the subconscious and conscious parts of your mind at war against each other.

Chapter Eight

Trauma Moments

Trauma is when pain exceeds capacity for joyful connection, and it seems as if the original painful experience has become locked in time diminishing one's identity.
—Father Andrew Miller

Trauma can occur for several different reasons. It can stem from recent events, or it can be rooted in painful childhood incidents. Some persons don't believe they carry residual pain while others are quick to face its damaging effects. Yet others have yet to identify the reason for their emotional struggles.

I think of trauma as a collection of small wounds inside us that prevent us from living from a place of wholeness. They fester because, although every child needs to feel love and affirmation, many lack the proper nurturing to overcome emotional assaults of any kind. Or, it could be the way we perceived certain circumstances that were never resolved, that created a negative impact.

Types of Trauma

James Wilder, a neuroscientist and coauthor of the book *The Life Model: Living From the Heart Jesus Gave You* writes about two traumas that can keep us stuck in past emotions.[10] They are Trauma A and Trauma B.

Trauma A can include the lack of good things like proper nurturing, the absence of supportive parents, or even feelings of abandonment. Perhaps parents were simply too busy making a living to provide for a large family to tend to a child's desperate needs. Maybe it was strictly the child's perception of events that left such deep and lasting scars. Many times, the problem was not overt abuse, but a lack of warm nurturing that parents need to give their children. When this is the case, it can be difficult to believe it made such a stunning impact that still affects us today. My own family fit that category, with an absent physician father and a socially prominent, busy mother. Trauma B can include more obvious abuse—anything challenging that happened to you: verbal or sexual abuse, humiliation, divorce, tragic losses, or bullying, to name just a few.

When children lack a sense of security because of the lack of parental connection and support, it leaves them unable to make healthy, stable connections with others later in life and may result in addictive tendencies. The psychological term is "object constancy," which is that safe bonding connection that happens early on in life—especially with the mother. Many families are just too busy to give the child that kind of needed attention. Without stable connections the child, especially from ages one to seven, forms mistaken perceptions and feels responsible for what happens in the family. They see mom and dad fighting and feel terrified that they will be abandoned. Or mom and dad divorce and they feel that they are to blame. The Lord wants to help us identify those early beliefs, so that they no longer control everything we do.

Some may mistakenly believe they had a *Leave it to Beaver* family life. That perception always raises questions in my mind because some families appear that way on the outside, but they may have things to hide on the inside. However, our fleshly nature alone can be responsible for the struggles or pain that may be unrelated to family dynamics. In Romans 7:15-17(NLT), we read that the Apostle Paul struggled to change because of the fleshly desires that controlled his inner man. "I don't understand myself at all, for I really want to do what is right, but I don't do it. Instead, I do the very thing I hate. I know perfectly well that what I am doing is wrong, and my bad conscience shows that I agree that the law is good. But I can't help myself, because it is the sin inside me that makes me do these evil things."

So how do we know that we're still being affected by past trauma? Many times, it can show up in self-sabotaging behavioral patterns—so that we do the very thing we want to stop. Or someone may exhibit child-like behavior because at a young age the emotions were ignored or suppressed. Consequently, natural emotional development never took place, so the person may still exhibit the behavior of a seven-year-old.

This scenario could result in ongoing marital conflict or discordant family relationships. It may reveal itself as a struggle for healthy marital intimacy. We may face a continual struggle with authority figures or addictions including alcohol or porn, or repeated failures when trying to build a business. It may show up as health problems. Research now indicates that those who experience childhood adversity are twice as likely to end up with cancer, autoimmune disease, or depression. As previously mentioned, we may exhibit emotional triggers that seem to be out of proportion which reflect back to earlier buried emotions. These emotions can result from subconscious programming of which we aren't even aware.

Researchers Bruce Lipton and Candace Pert have discovered how the body holds onto emotion that becomes coded in the cellular memory.[11-12] As discussed earlier regarding 9-11, when thoughts and feelings come into our consciousness the cellular memory causes us to perceive or behave in a pre-programmed manner.

The memory of the trauma is still there even though the event could have happened long ago. If it is grief over the loss of a loved one, it needs to be processed rather than stuffed and pushed aside. Otherwise, it never goes away and can show up in symptoms later. Other researchers have concluded that we have meridian pathways that are attached to specific organs. These pathways can be blocked due to repressed emotions. For instance, grief can manifest itself as lung problems, so that someone with unresolved grief issues will struggle to breathe. Or someone with unresolved anger may have liver problems.

As confirmation of such cell memory, we only must look at the number of transplant recipients who suddenly developed cravings or sensations that were contrary to their usual behavior. Researchers have concluded that the cells of the donor replicated the donor's characteristics once the organ was transplanted into the recipient's body. One recipient claimed that she craved beer and chicken nuggets, which, as it turned out, was the steady diet of the motorcyclist who donated her organ. The memory of that diet was deeply imbedded in the organ's cells. This information is from the book called *A Change of Heart* by Claire Sylvia.[13]

Scanning our Inner Terrain

> Our Shepherd is continually examining our inner terrain to see if there are any hidden strongholds that need to be uprooted and treated with His healing ointment.

In Marilyn Bay Wentz's book entitled *All We Like Sheep*, she says that when a shepherd suspects a problem with a sheep because of its failure to eat, he scans the sheep's body and parts of its wool coat, looking for abnormalities such as cuts or abrasions.[14] The scanning process keeps the sheep healthy and void of any ailment that may not be detected otherwise. She believes that this is exactly what our Good Shepherd does for us—continually examining our inner terrain to see if there are any hidden strongholds that need to be uprooted and treated with His healing ointment.

I recently experienced this situation in my personal life. I had already worked through many of my childhood issues, so I was quite surprised when some emotional upset unexpectedly manifested as intense feelings in response to being corrected by my husband. My reactions were far more intense than the situation warranted. One night he approached me about something as simple as a puddle of water around the toilet. I had created the puddle while trying to empty the water from a foot bath. I reacted with an intense feeling of rage. After I'd lashed out, I went to my bedroom, where my mind flooded with emotions. It felt good to release the pent-up emotions and face the real pain I was feeling. I realized that I had always held myself to an extra strict regimen of doing everything right, which was humanly impossible to maintain.

Later in the month, I was similarly shaken when a client said I hadn't handled things well in our session. That pierced a deeper place within me. Over time, the feeling rose again when there were other things I'd failed to do well. I realized that if God was trying to get my attention, He was doing a good job of it. With my emotions on high alert, I began to feel as if enemies were out to get me, and I was consumed with feelings of rejection.

Intellectually I knew that God was working for my good, but I didn't welcome the experience. It never occurred to me that maybe it was an answer to prayer. I had been praying that I wouldn't be controlled by the opinions of other people. Perhaps dredging it up was a way of getting to the source of pain so I could allow Him to heal my heart.

One weekend I was particularly determined to get to the root of the things I was feeling. I was journaling and seeking the Lord in this area when I asked Him to show me what was in my heart. In Psalm 139:23-24 David cried out "Search me, Oh God, and know my heart; Try me and know my anxieties; And see if there is any wicked way in me, And lead me in the way everlasting." I love the way David took a risk and invited the Lord to reveal what was in his heart, even after he'd fallen into sin.

As I sought the Lord, I suddenly remembered how paranoid my dad had been at times. He seemed to have continual thoughts that people were out to get him. It occurred to me that maybe I was being triggered by a generational stronghold that had been passed on from my dad's family.

I prayed to relinquish the generational stronghold that was on me. The following day I had a massage, but I still felt overly emotional. That night I attended a meeting at a ministry I've been involved in, and we prayed to receive the baptism of the Father's love. Later I realized that I hadn't fully embraced God's unmerited grace for me. I was surprised because I never feel that the Lord holds me to a standard of performance. It's just my own thing. But that explains why I tend to strive so hard to do things right, to feel worthy of the great gift of grace He offers me. In this process of discovery, I realized I was still trying to earn His favor though I was unaware of the cause until this recent upset brought it to my attention.

Not long afterward, I bought a book entitled *Baptism of Love* by Leif Hetland and began to devour it.[15] It's not the first time that I have read a book on the Father's love, but something seemed different this time. It felt as if the Holy Spirit was working more deeply in that area and I could no longer accept the lies I'd kept locked up inside. I felt a gradual lifting of the emotions;

even the paranoia lifted, and I experienced increasing freedom to accept the truth in my inner being that I am deeply loved. I recalled how the psalmist David said "I know that you delight to set your truth deep in my spirit. So, come into the hidden places of my heart and teach me wisdom." (Psalm 51:6, TPT)

Though my situation may not seem like a huge ordeal, to me it felt enormous. As I worked my way through this process, I realized that Jesus wants to pour out His tender love right when we need it most. He wants to flood us with love so we can receive His truth in the inner reaches of our hearts. I can now say that He is my Daddy. Because I had difficulty with my earthly father-child relationship, calling Him "Daddy" seemed to erase all the suffering of my childhood and replace it with His new-found love.

A woman recently shared that she was having a difficult time receiving the Father's love after being married to a man who continually belittled her, leaving her feeling worthless and inadequate. At that point, she didn't believe she could ever be good enough to deserve God's unconditional love. She regularly rehashed all her mistakes and felt she would never be worthy. My heart goes out to those who are stuck in this bind because they truly can't accept God as a loving father who offers grace for all our failures. In fact, He knew before we were born that we would be imperfect, yet He deeply loved us anyway. He never sits in judgment of us. Rather, He's there with open arms ready to welcome us with love and forgiveness. The story of the prodigal son illustrates this so beautifully. (Luke 15:11-32) The son who had gone off and squandered his inheritance was given a warm, enthusiastic welcome despite his past rebellious spirit.

A section that stood out in Leif Hetland's book *Baptism of Love* said this: "Jesus is not a mere 'hired hand' paid to watch over the flock. He declared He is the true Shepherd who will not hesitate to lay down His life for one single sheep." (See Luke 15:4-7.) No matter how devastating our life has been, He still waits for us just as He sought out the one sheep that strayed. No issue is too minor or insignificant if it bothers us. If we come to Him with a broken and contrite heart, He hears our prayers and wants to embrace us in our pain. We must simply surrender to Him what we are holding onto that prevents us from embracing the truth.

Only then we can reach out and drink from the well of living water, where every blemish can be released through Christ's blood that was shed on the cross. Through the stripes He endured on the cross, we receive healing for ALL of our afflictions. (See 1 Peter 2:24.) He is truly that Good Shepherd waiting to bring us to a fuller understanding of His love and the restoration He wants for His beloved ones.

Soul-Searching:

1. When you find yourself plagued with overwhelming feelings; do you identify by lashing out with anger rather than facing the vulnerable feelings?

2. Share the effect some early trauma has had on your life. In what way has this event caused you to repeat an unwanted behavior you can't seem to stop?

3. Disclose a time when you've been disobedient but were aware that the Lord welcomed you home with forgiveness and grace.

4. Can you identify an area in which an old emotional event was resurfacing strongly? Identify the feeling and the old circumstance it brought up. Can you imagine that Jesus was there with you in that situation, helping you heal and release those emotions?

Chapter Nine

Letting Go

*One of the most arduous spiritual tasks
is giving up control and allowing
the spirit of God to control our lives.*
—Henry J.M. Nouwen

J ust as sheep have difficulty following their shepherd, it's often difficult to trust the Lord with what we face each day, because as humans, we find security in assuming control of our lives. Many times, letting go feels like jumping off a cliff and wondering if anyone will catch us. We may feel that we'll be dropped into a dark abyss never to return, especially if we don't see God as someone worthy of our trust. It can be scary, so rather than trust the Lord to catch us we relentlessly hold on to control of any number of things including our husbands and children, our health, and even finances. Ultimately, we feel that it's better to hold onto our self-sufficiency than to trust the God of the universe with our well-being.

I am continually reminded of scriptures that command us to turn over our anxieties, our cares, and our control, so He can show us He will ultimately work things out for our good.

Anger with God

As we cultivate a closer walk with God and acknowledge that He is sovereign, in control of all things, we can become resentful that He doesn't orchestrate things according to our timetable. In the process, our resentment grows, so that we eventually get angry at God, though we can't admit it because we believe it's wrong. I've talked to people who say they can't get angry with God. But, just like with any other relationship we can build resentments that, like a wall, keep us at a distance from God. I happen to believe that resentment toward God is a sign we have a real relationship.

Some of the most intimate times I've had with God occurred when I wrestled with Him and shouted out my anger. It seems to release something, whether I write it out or just say it out loud. At that point, I notice that it's easier to embrace His love because the wedge of resentment is gone. I use a "feelings letter format" which is a great way to process such feelings. (I will go into more detail on this subject in Chapter 10.) Initially, the letter starts with anger and goes into what is behind it which reveals more vulnerable feelings. It can be quite helpful to direct those feelings toward God, to get to the actual root of the problem. Eventually, it leads to a place of acceptance where we can embrace true forgiveness and be open to real healing at the core level.

What does the Bible say about anger? Jesus grew very angry when He saw moneychangers in the temple courts cavalierly buying and selling and cheating others to get rich. He lashed out saying "My house will be called a house of prayer, but you have made it a den of thieves." (Matthew 21:13) He exhibited a great deal of righteous anger, even overturning their tables. But what about the times we feel justified in our anger and want to hold onto resentment toward the one who wronged us? We often feel that if we forgive, we'll be letting that person off the hook when they should pay for their actions. But that's like you are drinking poison and expecting the other person to die. In the end, that resentment only hurts you. When appropriate, I encourage people to write out their feelings so they can release all the layers underneath the anger.

> Unforgiveness is like drinking poison—it's poison to our souls.

We might have entered a covenant with our anger so that it's become our identity. In that case, we get some payoff from staying angry, which is why we don't move on. We might get more sympathy from empathetic ears, or we might feel justified in our disobedience. It becomes a way to support our decisions rather than look at what God is trying to stir up within us. Many times, it's a signal to see something that has triggered us, usually from unresolved childhood wounds.

Anger can be a protective mechanism, but many times there are underlying feelings of vulnerability, sadness, fear, shame or hurt. Anger can be used as a defense that prevents us from ever facing those root emotions. We can also use anger inappropriately to feel more powerful. I recently worked with a young woman with serious anger issues that surfaced whenever she felt she was wrong. Growing up, she experienced being bullied at school as she became a prime target for abuse. Recently she had episodes of rage when she would see her nephew, who was the same age she was when she was tormented at school. When she saw him, her anger became uncontrollable. This left her quite remorseful, because she loved her nephew and didn't want to respond in that way. As we talked, we identified a massive core of shame, which caused her to feel so insecure that she responded with overwhelming anger.

Sally experienced high levels of conflict with an adopted father who mistreated her and made her feel that she had to put up her fists to protect herself. Her father tormented her by constantly questioning his and his wife's decision to adopt her. As we worked on her childhood trauma, she realized that she had to be strong to protect herself from her sexually abusive birth father. Due to the early abuse, she had decided to be the "tough girl" so no one could take advantage of her. Consequently, her softer side had been stifled. The problems evolved into classmates perceiving her as unapproachable. The role she played covered the shame and anger she had hidden behind that hard shell.

Identifying the core issue is invaluable because lies that we believe can force us to use anger as a defensive weapon. I believe I was one of those who was unknowingly controlled by anger. I would lash out at my husband, who was wise enough to realize I was controlled by beliefs that didn't match up to my ideal image of a husband. It surprised me to learn that I had so many bottled-up feelings. I know that others saw me as a sweet, loving woman who would never raise her voice. However, repressed emotions can surface from inside us at the most inopportune times. They can occur when we haven't been able to express them in the past or haven't permitted ourselves to feel them.

What does Jesus think about feelings? Did He ever feel? It says in scripture that He experienced any number of normal human feelings as He was God in human form. He wept at the death of His dear friend Lazarus and he expressed righteous anger at the moneychangers in the temple. David faced a great number of fears and anxieties, many of which were based on actual physical threats. Moses was fearful of accepting the assignment to speak for God, saying, "Woe is me, I can't speak." I believe God is a compassionate Father who grieves over our losses and knows exactly what we're feeling. "For we do not have a high priest who is unable to empathize with our weaknesses, but we have one who has been tempted in every way, just as we are—yet he did not sin." (Hebrews 4:15) Abuse victims can be comforted to know that Jesus was with them early on, during every traumatic event. When I have taken people through a guided prayer time, I'm aware that Jesus always shows up in the memory with great compassion for what the child endured.

Ephesians 4:31 tells us "Let all bitterness, and wrath, and anger, and clamor, and evil speaking, be put away from you, with all malice." But before we can put it away, we need Jesus to validate our anger. Ask Jesus to show you how the anger looks. You might get a vision of a big ball that's red, full of fire. I've asked the Lord to see how my anger looked and was surprised about the image I saw. It was big with rough, jagged edges. Not a pretty picture.

Forgiving Heart

Once someone has worked through their feelings toward God, it's important to resolve any remaining unforgiveness. I make a point to warn people to not forgive too quickly because it can translate to merely using a Band-Aid® to cover feelings instead of working through and then releasing those feelings. I dealt with this issue years ago when I felt like forgiving my dad was the Biblical thing to do. However, I discovered later that I had multiple layers of anger that I had failed to process. To address this issue, I attended many healing workshops where I could express my anger in a safe environment.

Many feel that they aren't yet ready or willing to forgive because they feel that their abuser should somehow pay for what they've done. What did Christ say about forgiveness? When He was asked how many times to forgive, he said seventy times seven. (See Matthew 18:22) I often wondered why He responded that way. I gather that He wanted to make the point that we must be willing to repeatedly forgive those who have wronged us even if they aren't repentant. We are forgiven by the blood of the Lamb, so we need to practice that same forgiveness toward others.

I have often been struck by how Dutch Christian Corrie Ten Boom dealt with forgiveness for the ruthless behavior she experienced in the Nazi concentration camps. She endured so much grief in seeing her sister and father die. Fortunately, she was released from the prison camp due to a clerical error. Shortly afterward, she began a ministry of speaking worldwide about her experience. When she was giving one of her talks on forgiveness, she spotted a former prison guard in the audience. At the end of the talk she became apprehensive as she saw him advancing to her. He complimented her on such a fine message. He conveyed that he had become a Christian and knew his sins from the torture he put people through were all forgiven, however, hearing her message confirmed what he had experienced. Corrie was struck with an incredible coldness clutching her heart as he spoke to her.

As the former prison guard reached out his hand to ask her for forgiveness, she asked the Lord to give her the ability to forgive. As an act of her will, she reached out her hand to his, somewhat woodenly, and felt a current of love flow through her. She realized that she had been touched by the Father's love and was aware of the tremendous freedom of truly forgiving!

The hardest people to forgive can be ourselves. I can think of numerous times when I held onto something I had done and couldn't easily let it go. It would haunt me repeatedly with messages of condemnation. Once I was fully able to let it go, it lost its' hold on me. On the other hand, I've also discovered that we often put a Band-Aid on an open wound, thinking we have done the Christian thing by rushing to forgive others. This can only short circuit the process, so that we fail to experience the full range of feelings we need to see in order to completely release them.

Some recommend taking a bat and hitting a bed to let out the rage, but I don't think that's necessary. As I see it, we can make a tight fist and imagine the anger rushing through our bodies. Think of emotion as just another kind of energy, needing to move through our bodies. The more we feel it move, the more it surfaces, so we can deal with it and release it. I like to describe these emotions as waves. When a surfer starts out on a wave it's incredibly high, then it grows smaller until it dissipates onto the seashore. We need not be afraid of feelings, but rather we should allow them to move through the body the way a wave would. Before we ride the wave, we can cut through the faulty perception that created the negative feeling; once it's discovered and felt, it loses its power and shortly dissipates, so it no longer controls our emotions.

We can also release those feelings by putting them in the hands of Jesus. He's the Good Shepherd who wants to take all the heartaches we hold onto and exchange them for His peace. The apostle Paul encourages us to cast all our anxieties on Him so that in that place, He is able to guard our hearts. (Philippians 4:6-7) puts it this way: "Be anxious for nothing, but in everything by prayer and supplication, with thanksgiving, let your requests be made known to God; and the peace of God, which surpasses all understanding will guard your hearts and minds through Christ Jesus." (Ephesians 4:26) tells us: "Be angry, and do not sin: do not let the sun go down on your wrath."

There are various ways we can release feelings to bring healing. One way that I have seen people deal with them is to take their feelings to Jesus in an inner prayer session. We can ask the Holy Spirit to validate our feelings, allowing us to

diffuse all the shame we feel for holding onto the negative feelings. Then we can ask the Holy Spirit to show us how the anger
looks. We may get a visual image of the anger that might illustrate to us how massive it is. We can then ask Jesus to allow us
to release it and let it go. It's important to fully experience the
emotions, as it helps us move through them until they dissipate
and lose their power over us. To clear out the anger it may
also be beneficial to ask Jesus to help you get to the root of the
belief you formed.

You can also imagine that you are entering a courtroom
where you can bring God and Jesus into the room with you.
Following these steps can be helpful.

1. See yourself as a judge sitting on the bench.
2. Bring the offending party to the bench and begin to list
   the feelings and charges you have against that person.
   Notice where Jesus is standing to get a sense of how
   close or distant He seems to you.
3. Call Jesus forward and ask Him how He sees the offending party. Usually, you will hear that He lovingly accepts
   the offender. This process will help lead you to forgiveness as you see them the way Jesus sees them.
4. You can list and forgive each offense one by one: "I forgive you for ... until each one is released. Then you can
   tell the defendant that all charges are dismissed and the
   offender's record has been expunged.
5. Strike the gavel and finalize the decision in court. Turn
   the defendant over to the court of Jesus.
6. Look into His eyes and ask Him to forgive you for judg-
   ing the offenders.[16]

I have seen amazing results with the processes I have shared. Usually, the wall gets torn down, and we feel a greater connection with the Lord and His love for us. No longer do we hold onto the judgments as we speak and release them.

Soul-Searching:

1. Can you identify a role you have played that masked your vulnerable side, such as tough girl, nice guy, etc.?

2. What messages did you learn in your childhood that affected your level of comfort with expressing anger? How has this impacted your feelings toward God? Are you reluctant to express your anger toward Him, so you keep it bottled up? What result have you experienced after stuffing emotions?

3. How has holding unforgiveness given you a sense of empowerment when you didn't want to let someone off the hook? Think of someone you have difficulty loving or forgiving. What keeps you from releasing them? Explore ways to begin to let go of the pain and fully forgive.

4. What anger have you repressed toward yourself that is still controlling you? Have you been able to move into forgiveness toward yourself regarding past mistakes you might be holding onto?

5. Would you be willing to experiment with a way of releasing the anger and let Jesus take it away? If so, choose one of the methods listed and begin to practice it.

Chapter Ten
When the Physical Doesn't Work

It is through the power of the spirit
that miserable mountains are made
into fruitful plains.
—Bob Sorge

What happens when everything you try no longer works? You thought you were doing everything right, but somehow life events tumbled down to crush you. I had already written several chapters of this book, when suddenly the rug was swept out from under me. In hindsight, I realize that the Lord had a few things to take me through that would bring the subject matter to life.

My creative juices were fully satisfied before the bottom dropped out for me. I was doing my artwork, writing, and teaching a Bible study at church. But unfortunately, my body began to signal me with feelings of fatigue, confusion, and cloudy thinking, as well as memory issues. I began to make a lot of mistakes in my practice which left me feeling quite anxious because I wasn't on top of things. The anxiety level grew unbearable, and it wasn't long before I had trouble falling asleep. When I finally did, I would wake up intermittently throughout the night, facing my greatest fear—insomnia—that would prevent me from getting through the day the way a professional should. In the end, it left me feeling out of control, which was a problem because I've always taken pride in being well put together.

During that time, I felt very unsure of myself regarding my ability to function. I felt like a fraud. How could I effectively help others when I wasn't able to function? I used every method I could find for anxiety relief including deep breathing, stretching exercises, prayer, and the guided relaxation CD I had developed. I made sure my diet was very healthy and began juicing vegetables. It worked for the short-term, but the anxiety symptoms continued to crop up. I continued to hear the Lord say, "Trust me" and "Don't rely on the physical fixes that you usually use to deal with crises like these." I heard Him say that I needed spiritual rest more than physical rest. After all, I looked at my life and realized that I had become good at doing, and not very good at just resting in the arms of my Savior though I regularly recited Psalm 91 and pictured myself under the protective wings of Almighty God.

During that time, I took a class at a local non-profit organization where we learned how to effectively use the authority of Christ. I learned about binding and loosing whatever encumbrances we need to release. One night I had such an extreme head blockage that I didn't want to go to class. I felt God say to go ahead and go...that I'd probably get something I needed. When we prayed to bind and loose the enemy, I felt the release of a flood of tears, and surprisingly enough my blocked mind began to clear up. Then I felt the immense love of God flow over and through me. I left with a newfound trust and practiced putting on the full armor of God each day. I prayed that my brain would make the proper connections, and daily took on the full authority of Christ to bring healing.

When the symptoms continued, I spent some time with my friend from the non-profit who helped me get in touch with some family concerns that left me feeling very emotional. I released a big emotional charge that I had unknowingly held onto, and the symptoms subsided. It was at that time that I realized that strong negative emotions could manifest in physical symptoms that keep us in physical bondage indefinitely. It's not until we become aware of the issues that we can finally access healing.

I began praying that God would show me where I had held onto anything else from my past that might be affecting me. He led me to an old issue that I thought had been put to bed long ago. When I was in college, a guy robbed me of my innocence, after I had too much to drink. In that state, I was a prime target for his lustful desires for sex. I have never been able to handle alcohol well, and as a freshman in college, I was suddenly exposed to drinking for the first time. I loved the feeling of being uninhibited, but unfortunately, I ended up pregnant. As a result, I internalized a tremendous amount of shame that seemed unbearable. Because of my background, the worst thing I could have done was get pregnant out of wedlock. I told no one except my parents, who were very distraught and ashamed about what had happened. I decided to get an abortion as I didn't feel like I could face raising a child at that point in my life. I believe it created a lot of emotional distress and the beginning of some of my health problems. I had no idea how to deal with all the feelings, nor did I have any other sounding board.

Though I thought I had resolved those issues, years later I began to feel as if I had no control over anything. I couldn't control my sleep patterns, my anxiety level, or how I helped people. I had to be utterly dependent on God for everything!

I wasn't my usual productive self and spent many days just vegging out. For someone who likes to be busy with plenty to do it had been a nice reprieve for me, but not one without a lot of internal struggle. I questioned God, wondering why I had to go through this difficult process. But God reached down and told me it was all for my good—I just had to be patient with the process, because He was doing something very important in my heart and soul. I needed to be like clay and let Him be the potter. He began to show me that the way I had been living my life was contrary to the way He had designed me.

I tend to push for more and more of my physical desires, to control my husband and his choices, and to stay busy so I don't have to listen to myself, much less the voice of God inside me. The striving kept me in a perpetual state of do, do, do only to see that it was wearing me out physically, spiritually, and mentally. But more importantly, I saw that the greater benefit of healing came when I faced the fragmented parts of my soul. In my desperation, I have sincerely asked God to walk me through the feelings that surfaced. In that process, I discovered my great discomfort at being dependent and relinquishing control. As human beings, we struggle to let go of our self-sufficiency and be utterly dependent on God.

Recently our minister said that most of us need to face difficult challenges before we turn to God. It seems that in the absence of pain, we seldom see our need for Him. Early in life, we have been programmed to be strong and independent. If our parents were uncomfortable with their weaknesses or feelings, they might have taught us that this is the way to cope—simply by pulling ourselves up by our bootstraps.

I was very young when I began to read self-help books hoping to find answers regarding how to live. Unfortunately, they listed things to do to be better—like becoming more assertive and confident by making behavioral changes. I began reading the Bible the same way so that it soon became another series of do's and don'ts to live a happy, socially acceptable life. I remember reading Romans 12:9-21, which outlined a whole list of qualities we needed to incorporate to be "good Christians." I then tried hard to live them out so that I would be "good enough" to be accepted. Going to church only compounded the problem because I heard a whole new list of things to do in the church setting. However, I failed to recognize that if the heart is filled with unresolved wounds and resentment, no behavior will ever override the pain. At the time, I felt I must work harder rather than developing a healthy relationship that comes from a loving and accepting heart.

Over the years I realized that a residue of shame from my unwed pregnancy ending in an abortion still lurked in my subconscious mind. While my husband was out of town, I took a long weekend to focus on myself and do a feelings exercise that I give as homework to clients but rarely do for myself. It uses a letter format to write to someone, or even to yourself, to identify what you're holding onto that feels unresolved. It starts out with anger and then leads you through more vulnerable feelings. It is an outline of feelings you may be experiencing and eventually leads you to forgive that person. Even though I had worked on clearing these emotions numerous times, I felt that I still needed to forgive myself in some areas. Apparently, I wasn't allowing the forgiveness to penetrate the deep recesses of my heart. I decided to write the feelings letter to myself. Dear Suzanne... I'm angry because... I stayed with that first feeling long enough that I felt it was somewhat resolved before moving on to the next.

As I mentioned earlier, I'd learned early on in life that it was not okay to acknowledge or feel my emotions. Instead, I was taught to stuff them as if they would somehow magically disappear. Mother was always encouraging me to put on a happy face and get busy. She believed emotions weren't safe and had to be ignored—that they would ultimately lead us down a trail to unhappiness. When I was unhappy, I was taught to refocus my attention toward productivity. It wasn't until I got married that I realized that all negative emotions, especially anger, were okay to express if I didn't become controlled by them and take them out on others. Ephesians 4:26 says: "Be angry, and do not sin; do not let the sun go down on your wrath."

I have since come to realize that emotions are there for a reason and are God's way of communicating with us. He wants us to not only get in touch with our feelings but to release them healthily. When we fail to deal with our emotions effectively, they can get stuck inside our bodies where they stay buried indefinitely, and affect every area of our lives. As strange as it may sound, I've heard people say that what happened in the past does not effect them now. But I see this as a form of denial and resistance in those who don't want to face pain from the past.

Leaning on the Lord

To surrender fully, it seems as if it takes my health screaming at me to be in utter dependence on the Lord. Through the years this has been my greatest struggle and the method God uses to wean me away from my self-sufficiency. But, surrendering is not something I do easily. God is constantly teaching me that I need to trust Him and continually lean on Him. It's a new way of relating when I trust Him for everything moment by moment!

God uses these difficulties to take away my attachment to the external things that entice me and give me value. My pursuit of value from achievement gets squashed when suddenly my body doesn't support me as I push for more and more things to do. He has taught me a lot about being rather than always *doing*. Psalm 46:10 confirms that notion: "Be still and know that I am God." It's hard in this busy culture to just be still since everything promotes doing, doing, doing. Practicing meditation has been especially effective as I just sit, empty my mind, and wait to see what the Lord does. The biggest challenge is to silence all the voices of internal chatter.

When we stay focused on external things, it distracts us from feeling any negative emotions. That, coupled with "don't feel rules" with which we grew up, prevents us from fully embracing our feelings. At times we also look to the physical world to satisfy us through earthly pleasures that always fall short of the fruits of the spirit God wants us to have.

> **When we stay focused on external things, it distracts us from feeling any negative emotions.**

The most recent episode taught me that God wanted me to relinquish the façade of appearing put together, on top of my game. I had always felt the need to project the right image to others. But I'm aware that people can't easily relate to those who never struggle or reveal a human side. I was making blunders right and left, but somehow God still worked through me. He showed me that when I surrender my work to Him, He can do the emotional work in people, despite me.

That was a new realization that took the pressure off having to do my work in my strength.

The process of recovering has been quite a process of trusting daily. I continued to seek out the physical reasons why my body had gone through all that upheaval. I felt afraid because getting a good night's sleep was nearly impossible. I began to dread preparing for bed knowing that I might have a rough night ahead. I required a wide variety of supplements only to enable me to sleep intermittently through the night. When I cried out to God for answers, I found that He'd been leading me every step of the way. When I consulted a nutritionist, he tested me and determined that I had a bacterial infection, which explained why the dentist later found an abscess in my gums. I found that it greatly impacted my intestinal health, leading to increasing symptoms of anxiety.

I discovered through some blood work that I had also gone into a hyperthyroid state, which explained my weight loss of more than fifteen pounds. While I had always wanted to lose some weight, I found it frightening and confusing that it was happening without effort. It was not typical for me to lose a pound a week, so I realized something was wrong. At the same time, the naturopathic clinic I was going to had identified genetic mutations that affected my ability to absorb nutrients. That explained why the inflammation in my gut had affected every other system. They suggested nutritional supplements that gradually began to calm my anxiety.

During that time, I came to understand how Job must have felt when his world fell apart. When Job cried out to God, God replied that He was in control of everything and Job shouldn't question the Creator of the universe. In reading through Job, I realized how much I have resisted the notion of God's sovereign control over my life in the past. I reasoned that if He controls everything, why would a good and loving God want us to suffer? I recalled that Job regularly questioned God. "Why do I have to go through this?" God replied that He was in control of the universe, so Job need not question. As I read through the book of Job, I was aware that God was weaning Job from some inner pride. I realized that was probably the case for me as well. The lack of humility can be hard to see in ourselves since we can unknowingly make idols of what we think we need to have, be, or become. In our humanness, we struggle like Job to understand what's truly in our hearts.

During that difficult time, I was led to read the book *Hinds Feet on High Places* by Hannah Hurnard.[17] It's a wonderful allegory about the journey the Lord takes us through to purify us and transform us into His image. The author did a beautiful job using her creative writing style to illustrate what God wants us to experience on our journey. Toward the end of the book the main character "Much Afraid" received the new name "Grace and Glory" because of the transformation she'd undergone. One of the most important things she shared was: "I must accept with joy all that you allowed to happen to me on the way and everything to which the path led me." She describes herself as a little handmaiden full of "acceptance with joy."

We can be challenged to accept with joy what comes our way. Just like the scripture teaches us, we must choose to be thankful for all things especially when we don't feel it. I now trust that God will give me joy in the process if I truly surrender! I'm in awe of the transformation process we go through if we truly seek to submit to God, because our growth comes from a deep place of inner suffering which truly releases the things that hinder us.

As I struggled, I searched the scriptures for verses about sleep. I was directed to some favorites that I rely on. Psalm 23:1-2 (TPT) says "The Lord is my **best friend** and my Shepherd. I always have more than enough. He offers a resting place for me in his luxurious love. His tracks take me to an oasis of peace, the quiet brook of bliss." Psalm 127:2 says "It is vain for you to rise up early, to sit up late, then eat the bread of sorrows, For so He gives His beloved sleep." These have given me great comfort to know that He is able to provide the rest we need!

The greatest revelation came when I realized I needed to rest in the arms of the Good Shepherd, rather than to fill my life with things to do. Though I enjoyed those creative pursuits, I had focused on busyness rather than simply "resting in the Lord". My lack of sleep represented the true rest I was seeking and I had to give up striving to become something. True rest means I can fully receive His grace, knowing that I don't have to earn anything! It's a gift that requires no performance on my part. What freedom that brought to my life and work!

Soul-Searching:

1. Describe a Job experience where everything you tried to do no longer worked. What challenges did you face and how did you deal with them?

2. In what areas do you have trouble "resting" and trusting Him? Do you express your self-sufficiency by trying to make things happen in your own strength?

3. In hindsight, what good has come from a trial you experienced?

Chapter Eleven

Storms of Life

*Dear brothers and sisters when troubles come
your way, consider it an opportunity for great joy.
For you know that when your faith is tested,
your endurance has a chance to grow.*
—James 1:2-3 (NLT)

When sheep don't have an attentive, good master, they can become victims of neglect and die as a result. A good shepherd will give his sheep brandy and water to revive them. Just like sheep we need something to revive us when we become weak and stressed. Our Savior, Christ, is there to pour His redeeming and healing blood over us.

By the stripes He bore at the whipping post, His blood was shed for all our infirmities, pain, addictions, and depression.

What gets in our way is a lack of faith that He can be that kind of healer to us. We also need to know beyond a shadow of a doubt that He is right beside us, grieving with us in our trials. He doesn't typically remove the pain but is there to shepherd us through the process. My fleshly response is to be resentful and angry at God for allowing me to go through difficulties. But when I focus on being grateful, something is released in my spirit.

> What gets in our way is a lack of faith that He can be that kind of healer.

We may have a challenging marital partner and feel like nothing will ever change—or money troubles overtake us to the point where we doubt things will ever improve. Often, we fail to grasp what God is doing inside us, where He is working out things for our good. During my ordeal I regularly questioned God, asking if He was there or whether I would have to fight my battles alone. I often cried out to Him to relieve my severe anxiety, and I was encouraged when He was faithful to see me through each day. I saw how He engineered circumstances to prove that He was there working behind the scenes. At times I found myself weeping and experiencing fear I had never felt before. It seemed to consume me. I magnified situations in my mind that would never have bothered me in the past. I had thoughts of ending things but knew I didn't have the courage to take my life. Aside from the emotions that I was experiencing, I knew that God would somehow deliver me, but the big question was when? How long would He put me through it?

During that time, an author named Bob Sorge spoke at our church. I was drawn to his message because he talked about the journey through the pain that spoke right to my situation. He said that God takes us through captivity, to produce authority that He will use later in our lives. As the struggle goes on, He will weave a deeper, more beautiful story into the back side of the tapestry of our lives. He encouraged us not to waste the time during which God keeps us in captivity. Instead we should use that time to go deeper in the Lord, to pray more and to develop a stronger connection, so that we know beyond a shadow of a doubt that God is in the struggle with us. He is weaning us away from all the earthly attachments that hinder the growth of our spirit. He wants a bigger part of the real estate in our heart. But for that to happen, we must let go of the investment we made in earthly things that will never give us what He can, Bob said.

Bob recommended a book entitled: *Between the Lines: God is Writing Your Story.*[18] He shared his struggle when he lost the ability to talk after surgery on his vocal cords. And though God has not yet completely healed his voice, he continues to grow in faith and is faithful to share his journey with others.

Bob suggested asking God to help us see our trials through His eyes. And while I identified with everything he said, I struggled to wait on God to produce the growth. I was discouraged when I saw how long Old Testament believers had to wait for answers. David was in exile for ten years before God allowed him to rule as king. Other characters waited even longer. I believe it's key to have God's perspective on the waiting period while in the place of captivity. We have no idea what the Good Shepherd is weaving into our hearts through the period, which is why we must simply trust that the outcome and growth will indeed be good for us.

Love Penetrates

I tend to think that I need to orchestrate my life, and not to trust that God is in control even when I screw up. Through my struggles, I told Les that I finally realized that I can't control my life and that I needed the healing of Christ to truly release me from my bondage. One day when I was in my deepest, darkest despair, a friend came over to spend time with me. She left me this note which I believe she downloaded from the Lord:

"*Suzanne*: You are beloved, precious in My sight. You are beautiful. Your light shines for all to see. Your heart is pure, and I hold you in the palm of My hands. My Word does not return void but is everlasting. My angels surround you and protect you. You are a daughter of the most High God. My love for you is unfailing. You are not alone. You are loved, so let My peace abide in you."—*Your Father in Heaven*

When I read those words, I was extremely touched and wept tears of thanksgiving. Could it be that through this physical agony, God was deeply touching me with an even deeper revelation of the Father's love? He was clearly using this agony to allow His love to penetrate deeper into my heart because head knowledge could never saturate me enough to grasp His endless love for me.

I once heard the story of a girl who attended Columbine High School in Littleton, Colorado. Before she entered the school building on April 20, 1999, the day of the attack waged by two students, she prayed that the blood of Jesus would give her the covering of protection she needed. When one of the gunmen entered the school, she hid under the table in the library where he had approached students. From beneath there she called her Dad and let him know that an armed man had entered the school. He said, "Honey, I'll be there... Just wait for me." With much fear and trembling, she concentrated her thoughts on his words and remained hidden, waiting for him to come. But when her father arrived, he found the school completely locked down and barricaded, with no way to get to his daughter. Unbeknown to her, he had to go through the yards of nearby homes, jump over fences and spend hours trying to find a way into the building. But all the while he continued to stay connected to his daughter saying, "Honey, I'll be there." Her father finally arrived four and a half hours later, but by then the killer had left a bloody imprint on the library walls. Fortunately, she was spared. When her dad entered the room, she ran and embraced him in tears, finally safe in his arms. What a great example of our Father's loving commitment to protect us at all costs!

I have often reflected on the Father's Love Letter which is online at *www.fathersloveletter.com*.[19] When I read it, it's as if He's speaking directly to me. It appears that others like me must be in a place of despair to finally grasp the depth of the Father's love. When we can wholeheartedly receive His love for us, and accept the frustrating truth that our partner will never meet our deep love need, that our children will fail to reflect our loving parenting, or that our work won't give us the prestige we want, we can finally access His rest.

Marital Storms

One of the greatest challenges can come in our partner relationships. While one partner sees no need to work on his or her emotional issues, the other can be left feeling helpless to make any changes toward resolution. But we may be unaware that when we make changes in our own lives, it changes the dynamic between partners and can indirectly improve the relationship. Have you ever seen a mobile blowing in the wind? As one-part changes direction, all the other parts move in sync.

Every week, counseling offices are flooded with clients who want a behavioral fix to help them cope with marital issues. I have met clients in my office year after year only to find it extremely frustrating. Partners are usually reluctant to take responsibility for their part in marital issues, with the result being the blame game. I would often hear, "If my partner would just change, everything would be okay." I found myself listening to what "he did or said" and what "she did or said" only to be left with few effective strategies to help. It was clear that no one person was to blame. It was a two-way interaction where they were ping-ponging off each other and not taking responsibility for their part.

Les and I pray right away when we reach an emotional impasse in our relationship. If we seek God, then wait it out and endure the storm, God can do His amazing work within our marriage. I have seen God heal challenging areas, but it didn't come by changing my partner, but by changing me! I've come to believe that if couples trusted that God is big enough to heal them, there would be fewer divorces. I've discovered that by addressing my own issues, it shifts the dynamics in my marriage. I must continually recognize that my true partner is Christ and I am His bride. And when I look to Him to meet my deepest needs, He leads me through my darkest times, shining His light on me.

Soul Searching:

1. What life storms have you endured that have brought you to a deeper understanding of the Father's love? How did you learn to trust God in the process?

2. At what point have you endured a waiting period or a trial that felt indefinite? Have you later seen the new authority God gave you, because of the captivity?

3. Have you been able to grasp what God is doing inwardly with the discord in your marriage? What did you learn about yourself in the process? Have you discovered your part in the problems in your relationship?

Chapter Twelve
Family Expectations

The Spirit Himself bears witness with our spirit that we are children of God, and if children, then heirs— heirs of God and joint heirs with Christ.
—Romans 8:16-17 (NKJV)

I n my quiet time, I was intent on hearing from God. I asked the question, "What do you want to say to me?" It was Christmas time and every year at that time I feel a little depressed because we don't have much family in town with whom to celebrate the holidays. It feels like a lonely time even though I have a very loving, committed husband. We tend to plan a trip at Christmas to either visit people or take a break.

When I asked God this question, He said this: *"You make having family in your life too important. I am more concerned about weaning you away from the physical things you yearn for, so you can experience more of me. You just need to fix the eyes of your heart on the true family you have—Me within you. I am more valuable than any husband or family member you'll ever have. I always love and accept you. I am the author and perfecter of relationships and know just what you need. You need to embrace me more and not keep me at arm's distance. You need to come to me with your worries and put them in my hands."*

God wants to give us an internal family—Himself.

With that in mind, I've put much less emphasis on having family in my life. When I listen to people, I'm aware that many times their families cause all kinds of problems in their lives. It's made me more aware that it doesn't necessarily satisfy those inner longings. In fact, the Lord continually shows me that He can give me the good feelings I long to get through a family.

Recently I shared with a woman that God wants to give us an internal family—Himself. It doesn't have to be a human family, who will often fail to meet our expectations. The comforting truth is that He wants to fill us with everything we seek from a family. And that's true for many other areas as well. When I want something external to satisfy me, I need to go to Him with that desire and ask Him to fill me with the thing I'm missing; His fruits will give me the good feelings I seek. Through the dark days of my captivity, I learned to practice giving my needs to Him.

My heart grieves for those who struggle with family or marriage issues. Sometimes it seems that there is no other option but divorce. I am very much aware that separating isn't the best solution because it can bring much heartache for partners and the family. Biblically we're commanded to honor our vows, but sometimes when abuse is involved, it makes no sense to stay in a relationship that puts someone's life at risk.

Plank in Your Own Eye

Many individuals don't realize that marriage takes a lot of work. We may have idealistic views of what a marriage partner will give us—much like the movies portray. Both parties must be willing to listen to the emotions that the partner brings up in them. There are times God uses the marriage relationship to bring to our attention to the areas that stand in the way, preventing Him from producing His character in us. I believe it's His design to bring healing and wholeness as well as a stronger connection to Him. Scripture teaches: "Or how can you say to your brother, 'Let me take the speck from your eye;' and look, a plank is in your own eye?" (Matthew 7:4) We need to be willing to look inside ourselves rather than be so quick to notice what our partner is doing or not doing that doesn't meet our expectations.

Unfortunately, couples usually don't take responsibility for their own feelings, and they end up either stuffing them or lashing out on their mates or children. The resulting emotional explosions can lead to much pain and suffering that puts others at a distance. It keeps us bound in hateful behaviors that destroy any semblance of a loving partnership. There was a time early in my marriage when I was enraged that my husband didn't meet my expectations. Keep in mind that I grew up in a family full of doctors, with a father and grandfather who were good providers and considered successful role models in the community. In fact, I would frequently run into people who'd been delivered by either my dad or my grandfather.

I had chosen to marry a man from a background much different from my own. When his long-term sales career went south after 9/11, he sought various options that left him struggling to earn an income. As we endeavored to understand what God was doing, Les seemed confident that He was doing a deeper work in him—working on his arrogance, pride, and self-sufficiency. His success at selling long-term care insurance and becoming a national trainer had left him feeling quite self-sufficient and arrogant.

Les had made it a habit to ask God to reveal the things inside him that needed to go. In truth, he's probably the most soul-searching person I have ever known, and I've learned to respect His strong commitment to do the inner work that would allow God to transform him. He's a great partner for me because I needed someone who was self-aware and would take responsibility for his emotions. When both partners are willing to do the work, they can more easily work through many of their issues and resolve them.

However, I struggled to understand why God would keep him from making a living. I experienced an unexpected rage, assuming Les had done something wrong that caused his lack of sales. I had never seen such anger surface in me. As a result, I was faced with the stark truth, that I was not the nice, congenial girl I thought I was. Fortunately, Les allowed me to be angry and express it within reasonable limits, which was remarkable because I'd never been able to express that kind of anger in my family. Part of me was relieved to know I could get it out.

I regularly poured my heart out to God, asking for help to relinquish what I was holding. I went through multiple seminars that would help me release the pain by reliving some of the childhood feelings that were emerging. If we continue to stifle the child's emotions inside us, we never get past them or allow them to heal. As a result, they can later resurface at very inopportune times, because they're still in the subconscious ready to erupt at the next triggering incident.

Healing Marital Discord

I recommend that people keep a journal to express and share those feelings with God in a safe place. During that time, I used various tools that brought healing. One was a guided introspective process which I believed would help me release the feelings that had a negative hold on me. I walked myself through various childhood memories allowing Christ to be with me as that safe mentor and support. I began to discover that much of my anger was directed at myself because I was unable to meet my expectations for a successful career.

At that point all my early feelings of unworthiness, abandonment, and loneliness came flooding in. The feelings of abandonment stemmed from growing up with a father who seemed more attentive to his patients than he ever was to me. It left me feeling desperate for a father's love. I couldn't help yearning for that kind of attention from my dad. Also, my older siblings were busy with activities and had no time or interest in interacting with me. As a result, I was left feeling alone.

When I worked through early childhood feelings, I cleared out many negative feelings. Also, my fear of lack and scarcity surfaced when I realized I'd grown up amid great tension when the subject of money came up in our home. I remember overhearing angry conversations when older siblings wanted to buy a car, or my parents worried about losing money on investments. I found incredible freedom after resolving those emotions!

One day it occurred to me that I always used the word income rather than the word money. I found that significant. Maybe I was seeking more of the Lord's income of love and provisions to pour into me rather than seeking it from a human partner. Maybe I was also longing for that love and acceptance for myself. I began to realize that the outward anger was because I couldn't control the situation and I saw in Les a mirror image of what I saw in myself.

That kind of awareness can be very powerful if we can identify what the Lord is trying to draw out of us. My anger didn't subside right away, but I was willing to take a deeper look at the real roots. Throughout the process, I prayed regularly to see my husband through heaven's eyes. When we see through God's eyes, we may get an entirely different perspective.

Thankfully, the anger has now entirely dissipated. The process I went through had a great impact on me, so that I'm now convinced that He is truly the Good Shepherd who can restore our emotional life if we let Him. I released the image of what a husband should be to make me happy. Now I can honestly say that I can stand stronger in the identity Christ has given me, and I'm free to love my husband without seeking my value from him, instead of from God.

When counseling couples, I now know how vital it is to get to the deep root of issues, because without that, God is unable to transform our hearts, and we stay stuck indefinitely in our unproductive ways. He uses the conflicts we face to reveal deeper blocked areas—where He can begin the work or restoration. Many times, He uses methods that seem out-of-the-box. Some of these methods allow us to move through the feelings without suppressing them, because as mentioned earlier, they will tend to resurface later if we bury them.

> God uses the conflicts we face to reveal deeper blocked areas—where He can begin the work or restoration.

When we refuse to do the work to resolve our childhood feelings, we may stay stuck in the blame game, walking around with inner scars that we cover with Band-Aids hoping they'll go away. Thus, they never get resolved. At that point, we are truly those blemished lambs that need to drink from the Shepherd's well of redemptive power available for us.

Soul-Searching:

1. What disappointments created pain for you when marital or family relationships failed to meet your expectations?
2. At what point have you tried to get your identity from your children, or your partner's success?

3. Describe a time when you wanted to give up on a difficult relationship or marriage because you didn't trust that Christ could heal your despair.

4. Are you willing to look at your own heart and ask the Lord to reveal areas that are holding you back from being free to love effectively in your relationships?

Chapter Thirteen

Mirror, Mirror on the Wall

*Self-rejection is the greatest enemy of the spiritual
life because it contradicts the sacred voice that
calls us the 'Beloved.' Being the Beloved
constitutes the core truth of our existence.*
—Henri J.M. Nouwen

We come into this world in a fallen, imperfect state. Once Adam and Eve, we want to hide behind our external clothing to cover our blemishes. When Adam and Eve fell into sin, they chose to hide behind fig leaves. Due to our distorted images of ourselves and the media touting what is fashionable and beautiful, we grow up with tremendous pressure to maintain the kind of image the world portrays. We fail to accept our imperfections and find ourselves trying to cover them with clothing, makeup, and even plastic surgery so that we will look good for others.

I know I'm dating myself when I admit to growing up during a time when it was popular to be super thin. In fact, an extremely emaciated fashion model by the name of Twiggy was the poster child for that era. It's hard to believe that we young women all aspired to be very thin. No wonder it was hard to accept that I was a little plumper than average and to top it off, I had freckles and curly hair! Straight hair was so in vogue that I worked hard to straighten every one of my curly locks, which looked unnaturally severe and went against God's design for my hair. It's unfortunate how often we go against the way God has created us, to fit in or get the attention we so long for.

Growing up at a school where there was tremendous pressure to look good, along with a mother who was very focused on outward beauty and body image, only compounded the issue. Mother hid sweets in the kitchen hoping I would never find them. You see, back then I had quite a sweet tooth and regularly searched for treats in the backs of our cupboards. I was in junior high when I decided to join Weight Watchers, to prove to my parents that I could become the girl who fit their image of an attractive female. With no understanding of God's love for me, I aspired to lose weight until I found acceptance. My obsession with weight set the stage for many years of dissatisfaction with my body. Since then I've discovered that even though we drastically change our weight, we may still not be satisfied with our body image.

Achieving weight loss and undergoing cosmetic surgery may still leave us struggling to accept our flaws. Even after getting down to my ideal weight, I continued to find myself feeling discouraged. Fortunately, I can honestly say that now I know I'm beautiful in the Lord's eyes and love my body just as it is! I know I may be speaking to others who struggle with every imperfection. Either you are too short, too tall, wide around the midriff, your breasts are too small, or you have sagging skin around your arms. Not to mention your skin is too splotchy, your nose too crooked, and the list goes on. I know because I wrote the script and found it true, with men as well as with women. We can be very ruthless when we judge ourselves. We may also have endured the criticism or bullying of peers, which only made things worse. If those issues aren't dealt with in our youth, as we age, we still feel out of sync when we don't fit the currently acceptable mold.

What does God say about us? He never judges the color of our skin or hair, our weight, or the garments we wear. He loves us unconditionally and accepts every ounce of us just as we are. When the Lord sees us, He sees what is in the heart. He never designed any of us without inherent value. We all have gifts and an essence that is unique to us! But we must fully recognize and make them ours. All of us are beautifully designed by the Master who never makes mistakes. It was all in His plan! "I thank you, God, for making me so mysteriously complex! Everything you do is marvelously breathtaking." (Psalm 139:14, TPT)

I spent many years in the retail field where I was around beautiful models. When I would talk with them in the cafeteria, it was clear that behind those attractive faces were less than perfect lives. Beauty didn't make them exempt from pain or struggles; it quickly became apparent that very few of them were truly happy inside. As I follow movie stars who are revered for their talent and looks, I'm always amazed at how often their personal lives are in shambles.

The sad truth is that most of us refuse to accept what we consider flaws and imperfections. There is a saying that what we resist persists. I like to describe it as trying to pull a finger through a Chinese finger trap. What happens when we put our finger into the woven tube? It gets stuck in the tube, unable to be released. This illustrates how hard it is to find freedom when we continue to hold onto control. Once we cease the pressure and allow the woven tube to release, the trapped finger is easily removed. This example demonstrates how we deal with appearance and especially weight challenges. First, we must accept where we are and not resist. If we allow the Lord to give us value and let go of control, we can feel His anointing oil restore the beauty of our essence. He heals all our internal blemishes, so we're no longer controlled by those on the outside.

In this process, it's important to watch the words we speak to or about ourselves. Are they affirming or belittling? Our words either build us up or tear us down. Proverbs 18:21 tells us: "Death and life are in the power of the tongue." It continues to say that we become what we think and speak over ourselves—a self-fulfilling prophecy. So, learn to be your own best friend by making positive declarations that will build you up instead of death words that can ultimately be your undoing.

I was reading the book of Ephesians this year, and chapter 2:10 stood out: "For we are God's masterpiece. He has created us anew in Christ Jesus, so we can do the good things he planned for us long ago." Other translations say we are His workmanship. I had always focused on the good works He was preparing us to walk in, skipping over the notion that we are His masterpiece. I love reflecting on that! I use the following affirmative statements to program my mind to agree with what God says about me. "I am beautiful in the eyes of the Lord. I am His Masterpiece! I love and embrace my body's shape and design."

> **Just bask in the truth that you are purely loved and seen as beautiful, without any external attachments.**

Can you look in the mirror and say you absolutely love your body? I have asked people to do this as an exercise in the nude without clothing. I know that's a stretch, but it can open you up to accepting your body in the natural state without the covering of fig leaves. I find it incredibly interesting how most people are instantly drawn to their flaws and see nothing else. Why is it that we can't we see our essence or the God-given traits that make us attractive to the Lord? When I think of people whose company I enjoy, it's rarely because of their outward beauty. It's usually their genuineness, authenticity, sincerity, or compassion that draws me to them. It boils down to their ability to be real and not project a false front. I'm truly attracted to those who aren't afraid to be themselves.

While you're still looking in the mirror ask the Lord to show you how He sees you—without any blemishes, pure and flawless in His eyes. He might give you a visual image or impression. Just bask in the truth that you are purely loved and seen as beautiful, without any external attachments.

Lessons from Canvas

One of the gifts that I have developed is my artistic ability. My dad took up acrylic painting in his later years, and he has always encouraged me to do the same. He felt that some talent ran in the family and that I should explore painting, so I decided to take watercolor classes. I've found that I love the right-brained expression and process of pouring out colors on a page and seeing how I can express my essential self.

I found a great instructor nearby and sheepishly signed up for my first class. I'll never forget my first project: applying masking fluid to a drawing before we started with the watercolor paints. It started out on a challenging note when the container slipped out of my hands and landed on the floor soaking my coat, sweater, and purse! The fluid is much like rubber cement when it gets on something. Within a matter of minutes, my clothing was completely covered with this sticky fluid that's not easy to remove.

The incident literally had me in tears! I already felt ill at ease about trying something unfamiliar, and the spill only added to my angst. One of my classmates reassured me that it would get better. She said everyone feels uneasy when starting something new, especially in the presence of others who are more experienced. I wondered if I should continue with the class since I'd already failed at the simple task of masking. I rushed to clean off the spilled substance but found that a struggle, because it really stuck tight. It was a good reminder of the way we try to mask our facial scars and wrinkles, or cover our bulges with loose, dark clothing. Or, we may let others' opinions spill over us coloring our true view of ourselves and find that just as difficult to shake off. That kind of negativity can leave us unable to receive the love Christ wants us to embrace. He wants us to see that we can put on the unblemished cloak of His righteousness in a world tainted by fallen people. We simply must not allow those fiery darts to penetrate.

The other valuable take-away from the class was that each student would express the very same drawing in their own way so that each painting was uniquely different from the others. Whenever we completed a painting, the instructor would place each one on display and critique them. I was always a little reluctant to allow mine to be put up for viewing but was eager for the instructor's constructive criticism. Isn't that how we should feel about Christ? We should give Him our blemished internal images and ask Him to reveal whatever is out of alignment with His plan. Then He can give us what we need to feel okay about ourselves in any given situation. In the end, we don't have to be plagued with feelings of self-doubt, inadequacy, or shame since we can experience the Good Shepherd's perfect acceptance.

Soul-Searching:

1. How have the media, family messages, or peer labels affected the way you feel about your appearance? Share how such messages are impacting the way you relate to those around you.

2. Allow yourself to fully accept yourself without shame: your body, your appearance, your personality. Breathe in deeply as you look in the mirror and see what the Lord

will show you. What good things do you see when you focus on God, instead of looking for flaws? Practice some affirmative statements as you view your true self, no longer hiding the real you.

3. Have there been times you let others color the way you feel about yourself by taking on their negative judgments? Did you grow up with a parent who was quick to notice and mention your flaws?

4. Have you tried to mask your true beauty with outward fixes only to be left disappointed that the results did nothing to change how you feel?

5. List the unique character traits God has given you. Write them down and share them with someone you trust. Ask them to give you feedback about what they see.

Chapter Fourteen

Lies We Believe

Repentance is a change of mind that leads to a changed life as we see the reality of our sin in the light of God's love. Repentance is not simply about just saying 'no.' It is also about saying 'yes' to the gift of the Father.
—Neil Lozano

As a child Suzy wondered silently, *"Why doesn't anyone listen to me?"* She eventually found herself pounding on the dinner table saying, "Let me talk." Suddenly all the adults and older siblings turned to her saying, "It's Suzy's turn to talk." Unfortunately, she found that she was tongue-tied and started speaking gibberish, once she was put on the spot to speak.

Fast forward fifty years. Today she still wants others to know she has a great deal to say. She gravitates toward the idea of public speaking because then she'll have a captive audience to listen when she speaks. She travels in social or church-related circles, taking a backseat to others who are more vocal and engaging, too caught up in their own little worlds to imagine how very much alone she feels in a world that caters to extroverts.

I am Suzy—that's the name I used until I graduated from college. The dinner table memory has been one of those defining moments—a focal point that's colored my outlook throughout the years. It left me feeling ignored and overlooked. How do you react when you feel devalued? Perhaps you push yourself even harder to perform, believing that people will recognize your great talents and want to be with you. What tends to escape our understanding is that there is one Person who always recognizes our greatness—God!

The Lord Jesus never overlooks or ignores us. In fact, Scripture says He inclines His ear to hear when we call. He's available every moment of every day, eager to give us the complete love and acceptance that we so long for. We tend to look for love and acceptance in the wrong places—from people, achievements or leadership roles. We become people pleasers, perfectionists, or even narcissists to fill the tremendous void inside us. Hebrews 4:16 says: "Let us then approach the throne of grace with confidence so we may receive mercy and find grace to help us in our time of need." When we make a practice of going to Him, He's promised to minister to the need of the moment as no one else ever could.

If there's one common factor I see in most people, it's that they feel unworthy of the value God gives them as His cherished treasures. We wander around like wounded soldiers unable to hold up our heads and walk in our true authority and identity. We may believe we don't deserve healing for the soul wounds that keep us in bondage from our past. We have buried childhood memories that shout lies, saying we'll never measure up, or that we aren't lovable enough to receive the great gifts God has for us.

Hearing His Voice

Many times, traumatic events have set us back, resulting in a defeatist mentality. We don't see how we can overcome what seems like a doomed marriage, a significant job loss, or a child with major problems for which we feel responsible. What we believe can keep us in bondage to those lies that we're "not good enough." Those beliefs can rule us and cause us to feel stuck, unable to believe that Christ can impart His truth into the inner crevasses of our soul and change everything. They might even show up in vows that I must do something, which can be much more powerful than our other beliefs, ultimately shaping our view of ourselves and dictating our behavior.

I believe we need to find scripture promises that we can claim as our own, tucking them deep in our hearts. There's something powerful about hearing the voice of God so He can erase many of the lies we believe. In John 10:27, Jesus said, "My sheep hear My voice, and I know them, and they follow me." He goes on to say, "And you shall know the truth, and the truth shall make you free." (John 8:32)

In the John 10 passage, the author describes Jesus as the Good Shepherd who gives His life for His sheep. Jesus contrasts

Himself with the hireling who is not attentive to his sheep and is quick to abandon the flock when danger comes.

This description reveals the tremendous commitment Jesus has made to be a Good Shepherd who never leaves us. The passage goes further to say that "He lays down his life for his sheep." That is incredibly comforting and hard to fathom in a world where commitments are often made and broken. Many make commitments over handshakes but never follow through.

Marriage vows are made because it's a tradition, with no guarantee that both parties will stick it out if life presents tough challenges. I recently ran across an article that listed male celebrities with photos of their first wives and then mentioned the marriages that followed. Only one out of the twenty men had been widowed and had a remarriage that lasted! It saddens me to see how fame and fortune can rob people of commitments that in the end, didn't last.

Buried Emotions

I've spent years trying to reprogram my mind to believe what God says about me in His Word. "I can do all things through Christ who strengthens me," or "I am made new in Christ... old things have passed away." For some reason, they didn't seem to penetrate deep enough to produce any significant transformation. It wasn't until I discovered that deeply embedded emotions could be held captive in my body and that I could escape their captivity if I could identify and release them. Emotions that we don't accept, express, or release get stored as repressed energy. I have repeatedly seen that negative emotions end up buried in the body, where they can color the way we feel about ourselves.

The root of such issues can often be traced to feelings of shame or unworthiness.

Since they are filed away in places unknown to our conscious minds, they keep us in emotional bondage and prevent us from owning our true God-given identity. His deepest desire is that we believe and receive the significance He has given us. Too many believers feel less than deserving of such a wonderful gift, and do not believe they are truly beloved children of the Most High God. So why can't we truly own that and walk in confidence knowing that God means what He says?

Many determine their worth by the way they think others see them, much like giving someone a blank price tag and asking them to write down what we're worth. In that way, we become people pleasers and want other people to give us the value that God has already destined for us to have. I regularly recite Romans 8:31: "What then shall we say to these things? If God is for us, who can be against us?" As I declare that truth, it has begun to saturate deeply into my heart. I also like to recite an affirmation "I am important in God's eyes and to myself no matter what people think."

God is a master gardener, and He wants to help us weed out the old faulty lies that control how we see and feel about ourselves. We need to literally "put off our old self," which requires a *decision* on our part. "That you put off, concerning your former conduct, the old man which grows corrupt according to the deceitful lusts, and be renewed in the spirit of your mind, and that you put on the new man which was created according to God, in true righteousness and holiness." (Ephesians 4:22-24) Following are some of the declarations I now refuse to speak over my life. Most reflect lies that prevent us from fully adopting the identity God has designed for us.

> We are beautifully designed by the Master who never makes mistakes.

Ungodly Beliefs about Myself

Theme: Rejection, Not Belonging or Fitting In

1. I don't belong. I will always be on the outside (left out).
2. My feelings don't count. No one cares what I feel.
3. No one will love me just as I am for being myself.
4. I will always be alone, and no one is there for me.
5. I will withdraw and isolate myself so that I won't feel rejected.
6. I never fit in or feel accepted by others.

Theme: Unworthiness, Guilt, and Shame

1. I am the problem when something goes wrong. It's always my fault.
2. I'm not lovable.
3. I must wear a mask so that people won't know the true me.
4. I've made many mistakes for which I always must pay the consequences, and because of them God won't bless me.
5. If I had only been a better child, I would be loved.
6. I can never do anything right.
7. I'm a burden.
8. I'm a mistake and should never have been born.

Theme: Performing to Achieve Self-Worth, Value, and Recognition

1. I am not valuable if I'm not needed.
2. If I don't perform well, people won't see me as worthy.
3. I don't speak up for fear that others will not approve of me.
4. I have no voice to be heard.

Theme: Control to Avoid Hurt

1. I can't relax if I can't control things.
2. I don't feel peace within if I'm in conflict with others.
3. I need to have others do what I want, so I feel in control.
4. I don't feel safe in this world.

Theme: Physical Appearance

1. I feel unattractive, as if God somehow shortchanged me.
2. I can't lose weight and am stuck with this body.
3. I dislike my body and never feel good about my sexuality.
4. I crave foods that nurture me but aren't healthy for me.

Identity Themes

1. I should have been a boy (girl), so my parents would value or love me.
2. If I am true to myself, people won't appreciate me.
3. I can never measure up to what God wants me to be.

Personality Traits

1. I am an angry (shy, jealous, insecure, fearful, etc.) person.

Prayer of Confession for Ungodly Beliefs

1. I confess my sin (if appropriate and my ancestor's sin) of believing the lie that_____.
2. I forgive those who have contributed to my forming this UGB (ungodly belief). (Be specific.)
3. I ask You, Lord to forgive me for receiving this UGB, for living my life based on it, and for any way I have judged others because of it. I receive your forgiveness.
4. By your forgiveness, Lord, I choose to forgive myself for believing this lie.
5. I renounce and break my agreement with this UGB. I cancel my agreement with the kingdom of darkness.
6. I choose to accept, believe, and receive the GB (Godly belief) that_____.

By praying this simple prayer of confession, you can unleash yourself from many of the faulty belief patterns that prevent you from living the abundant life. The enemy of this world would love to keep you stuck believing lies, so don't allow Him to deceive you! It is then vital to affirm the godly beliefs, so you leave no opening for the accuser to come in. Matthew 12:43-45 says that when we don't replace the negative beliefs, Satan can enter with seven other spirits! We need to replace that mindset, leaving no opening whatsoever.

Godly Beliefs about Myself
Rejection, Not Belonging
1. I belong and am adopted into to the kingdom of God.
2. My feelings count and are important to express.

3. I am loved unconditionally by God. Those who are close to me can allow me to express whatever I feel.
4. God is always with me, and I will never be alone.
5. The Lord gives me safety, so I can be open and connect honestly in relationships.

Unworthiness, Guilt, and Shame
1. I am worthy because I am a child of the most high God.
2. I am lovable.
3. I am accepted, forgiven, and washed clean by the blood of the Lamb.
4. I can be open and honest with others because God redeems me.
5. I am loved and accepted just as I am.
6. I do my best and leave the rest to God.
7. I am a sweet aroma and blessing to others.

Performing to Receive Value and Recognition
1. I can be appreciated and recognized for just being myself.
2. I am valued and appreciated for who I am and not just for what I do.
3. I speak my voice and share my opinions regardless of what others think.
4. I am fully approved by God because He doesn't measure my success.

Control to Avoid Hurt
1. God provides rest in my spirit.
2. Peace abides in me even amid conflict.

3. I trust God for His control of others.
4. I am safe and secure in God's hands.

Physical Appearance
1. I am wonderfully made according to God's perfect design.
2. I love and accept my body the way God created it.
3. I embrace my sexuality and am free to express it.
4. I nourish and nurture my body with foods that are healthy and healing.

Identity Themes
1. God values me regardless of my gender.
2. I am fully accepted living from my authentic self.
3. I am given grace and acceptance because I am a new (wo)man in Christ.

Personality Traits
1. Angry—When anger arises, I am okay releasing it and allowing God's peace to abide in me.
2. Shy—I receive boldness from God.
3. Jealous—I can be content because I have everything I need.
4. Fearful—God is love and has not given me a spirit of fear but power, love, and a sound mind.
5. Insecure—I am confident in the value God has given me to live out His purposes and plans for my life.

Soul-Searching:

1. Think back to a defining moment that revealed self-sabotaging behaviors in yourself. What do you believe is causing the behavior?

2. Are there ways you have built up walls that limit you from truly hearing from God? If so, can you ask God to help you identify what belief is creating the wall and how He wants you to break it down?

3. Have you ever experienced listening prayer where you asked God to show you something, and He answered you? If so, describe what happened and what you heard.

4. From the list of ungodly beliefs above, choose some faulty beliefs of yours that have affected how you feel about yourself. Would you be willing to go through the confession prayer and release them? Take time to journal them as the Lord reveals and find a partner to support you as you walk through the simple prayer of confession above.

Chapter Fifteen

A Renewed Mind

If you are not thinking right, if your mind is not being renewed, if you are not focused on God and His Word properly, it will show up in your emotional life.
—Neil T. Anderson

A re we willing to let the old negativity be pulled out and put new wine into new wineskins? (See Matthew 9:17) This scripture indicates that to be preserved, we must first clean out the old wineskins (negative thoughts) before placing new beliefs in new wineskins. For the old attitudes to be cleared out, we must be willing to surrender every aspect of ourselves to God. The Apostle Paul says: "I beseech you, therefore, brethren, by the mercies of God, that you present your bodies a living sacrifice, holy, acceptable to God, which is your reasonable service. And do not be conformed to this world, but be transformed by the renewing of your mind, that you may prove what is that good and acceptable and perfect will of God." (Romans 12:1-2) That doesn't mean just giving Him parts of ourselves, but rather our whole selves. As we submit ourselves to God, our minds will gradually be renewed.

Mental Focus

Our minds are powerful because they influence every molecule of our being. Our thoughts can bring us to destruction. We make choices every day regarding where we want to focus. If we focus on lack, we see all that is missing. If we focus on abundance, our thoughts go to everything that is good in our lives. Paul encouraged the Philippians to meditate on what is true, noble, just, pure, lovely, and good report. (See Philippians: 4:8)

Caroline Leaf, a communication pathologist and audiologist working in the field of cognitive neuroscience, wrote an interesting book entitled, *Switch On Your Brain*.[20] Her book is full of research that explains how we can detoxify our brains from toxic thinking by creating new neuropathways that can influence our emotions and even transform our DNA! She calls this neuroplasticity which the scripture refers to as the renewing of our minds. (See Romans 12:2.) The exciting thing is that new thought patterns form in 21-day cycles, and when we diligently focus on the new thoughts for that relatively short length of time, new connections form in the neural networks of the brain. She then challenges us to discipline ourselves to stay the course, trading old thought patterns for new, to get a brand-new start.

The Bible says that we can daily benefit by taking our captive thoughts to Christ. "Casting down arguments and every high thing that exalts itself against the knowledge of God, bringing every thought into captivity to the obedience of Christ." (2 Corinthians10:5) We must be cognizant of what we think lest negative thoughts become a stronghold in our minds, and we spiral down before we get a chance to surrender them to the Lord.

I've discovered something interesting. If the fuel driving the thought process isn't released from the subconscious, it may take even longer to get rid of, which is why it's so vital to continually reprogram the mind with new truth. Once the root of the issue becomes apparent, new and anointed revelations and godly thoughts can be embedded into new brain pathways. Many people think of these as affirmations, but I like to call them declarations. Even if you're not quite persuaded that they're true, you can still declare them as truths. Applying the truths from scripture can be very powerful since the Word of God never returns void. (See Isaiah 55:11.) It's not enough to just speak these declarations silently because power is released when we speak them out loud in faith. God will not break a covenant with us when we've declared the Word aloud. "My covenant I will not break, nor alter the word that has gone out of My lips." (Psalm 89:34). Look up scriptures that are applicable and speak them out loud as a regular daily discipline. These scriptures can be especially helpful when we're trying to break through regarding the Father's love for us.

When old toxic thoughts lift their ugly heads against you, you can command the enemy oppressors to leave, because Jesus died to defeat them with His blood, which is why they no longer have the right to speak lies to you. I have a whole list of these scripture references that I declare as truth especially when I am feeling emotionally down. Declarations are not asking God to do something, but rather speaking the truth of God's Word out loud to send the enemy running for his life. My favorite is: "For I know the thoughts that I think toward you, says the Lord, thoughts of peace and not of evil, to give you a future and a hope." (Jeremiah 29:11)

As I see it, the enemy's greatest challenge is to break down and destroy our identity and authority. As I mentioned earlier, the belief that we're "not good enough" is hard to miss in nearly everyone. It's so predictable that I can almost write their script before we discuss what's blocking them. We can all see the fleshly parts of ourselves that are a carryover from the fall of Eve that speak to the issue of value and condemn us so that we must run to God with the "not good enough" syndrome.

> The enemy's greatest challenge is to break down and destroy our identity and authority.

But the reality is that we all need to put on the cloak of His righteousness that has been imparted to us through Christ. Even though our hearts are deceitful, our new nature can truly receive what scripture says belongs to the "new man." "Therefore, if anyone is in Christ, he is a new creation; old things have passed away; behold, all things have become new." (2 Corinthians 5:17)

We often camp out on problems with our "old man" and are unwilling or unable to believe we have a new nature. It's that selfish, fleshly part of us that doesn't believe the truth. That's the part of us that needs the daily renewal exercises.

We can clear out these energetically using a tapping method called Emotional Freedom Technique (EFT) which was developed by Gary Craig who observed Dr. Roger Callahan, founder of Thought Field Therapy.[21] Gary further developed the method and then used it in his own EFT process. Dr. Jim Richards has applied this process to a Biblical Christian framework. While some clients have difficulty believing this can work, others have gravitated to this tool as a way of clearing out their hindrances. When I was introduced to this technique, I didn't believe it would transform the thoughts that controlled me. In my graduate counseling program, I learned all the principles of psychology, so the EFT process seemed too simple to be effective. I was amazed by the results! I believe it's powerful because while tapping on a sequence of acupuncture points, you speak aloud a declaration of love and acceptance of yourself, even while facing your problems. When you have made several rounds of tapping on an issue, then you can tap on an affirmative belief. The healing tends to be permanent, much like removing a thorn from a cactus, as those thorns cannot grow back.

An example would be that you get overly anxious when signs of conflict are on the horizon. This uneasiness might be created by your partner or a co-worker, and you want to withdraw rather than face it directly. To apply this practice, you need to rate how intense the feeling is on a scale from 1 to10, with 10 being the highest.

Then you can start a tapping method on designated acupuncture points with a repeated phrase that goes like this: "Even though I'm feeling anxious and my temptation is to withdraw from the conflict with ___, I deeply and completely love and accept myself."

After going through a round of this and seeing how you feel, you can then go through another statement saying: "Because I deeply and completely love and accept myself, I choose to overcome anxiety and not withdraw from conflict."

The last repeat phrase will be this: "Because I deeply and completely love and accept myself and I am totally loved by God, I am filled with strength and courage to move toward conflict." Once you have gone through these three rounds of statements, you can rate yourself again where you fall on the scale. The goal is to get to zero, so that you are neutral with the anxious feeling. If you are at peace with this issue, then you no longer need to tap. I have used this tool continually and seen fast results. The beauty of this is that you can use it on any negative feeling you are having. The next time you bump up against an impasse in resolving a feeling, simply apply this method and see how you feel. See Dr. Richards' website www.impactministries.com for further clarification. Another great resource is www.glorywaves.org/products.

Voices of Self-Compassion

I talk a great deal about our relationship with God, but one of our most vital relationships is the one we have with ourselves. I find that once we truly understand the love of the Father, we need to relate to ourselves with that same kind of compassion.

That's where it can be challenging. If our self-talk condemns us, it can override the immense love God wants to pour out on us. The Father's voice is never condemning, but rather always affirming, even when He corrects us. The voice of condemnation we hear is from the internal demons whose lies we believe to be truth.

To stay on top of the situation, we should consciously examine our self-talk daily. Are we speaking condemnation or love and affirmation?

In researching this issue, I found the website of Dr. Kristen Neff, a researcher, and professor at the University of Texas at Austin. She runs what she calls a self-compassion lab where she offers a self-compassion assessment that helps readers identify areas where they struggle to be kind to themselves. Her website can be found at *www.self-compassion.org*. In her book, *Self-compassion: Stop Beating Yourself Up and Leave Insecurity Behind*, she identifies three elements that are essential to be compassionate with ourselves. They are self-kindness, common humanity, and mindfulness.[22]

Self-Kindness: Being warm and understanding toward ourselves even when we fail or feel inadequate.

Common Humanity: Common humanity recognizes that these feelings of inadequacy are something we all go through. It is not just what happens to "me" alone."

Mindfulness: Mindfulness means that we don't over identify with feelings by magnifying or suppressing them.

There was a period during which I found myself repeatedly cutting myself with a certain kitchen knife I used. It happened so frequently that it captured my attention and made me wonder if it was a message I should investigate. When I prayed, the Lord showed me that it was a metaphor for my cutting myself down. Only the Lord could have helped me make that connection. I decided from then on to be gentler and more compassionate with myself, especially after making mistakes. It was only a short time later that I realized the episodes of cutting had greatly diminished.

When working on self-compassion, it helps to imagine ourselves as two-part beings, a present self, and a younger self. Our younger self is the one with emotions that are often overlooked or ignored, rather than recognized and validated. Consider the way you would talk to a child. Would you use a harsh tone of voice, condemning messages or judgmental attitudes? Hopefully not. Just as children's feelings need to be supported, we must allow the vulnerable child inside each of us to be heard and validated and let him/her know that we are there for them and we care about their feelings.

Listen to your faulty thinking patterns— "the all or nothing," "the catastrophizing" or the "what ifs." In fact, the "what ifs" can either lead us down a destructive path or a hopeful one. Many times, they exist only in our minds and never happen. However, our perceptions are very powerful and can greatly impact the way we respond to challenges. Researchers have determined that the brain can't distinguish between what is real and what is imaginary, which means that if we visualize ourselves accomplishing something or our body healing with little Pac-Men consuming unhealthy cells, it can have a powerfully positive impact on our well-being.

If we choose not to focus on "what if" (the worst possible outcome), we can believe God's promises and visualize a positive outcome. I like to use this option to deal with the personal struggles I face. If I can begin to see the good outcome that God may be weaving into my life, it can make it easier to endure the trials I face. Then I can truly embrace Him as the Good Shepherd who is working things for my good in whatever situation I encounter.

From the Head to the Heart

Believe it or not, it's possible to have an irreconcilable contradiction between what the head and the heart believe, especially when a child's family does not feel like a safe place to be. When this is the case, children learn to live in their heads to protect themselves. It's the ultimate survival mechanism and can be the only way to make sense out of the chaos they experience as children. But living out of the thinking center can prevent us from dealing with feelings that may not be trustworthy. As a result, it may feel safer to simply analyze things and never feel emotions at all. The outcome is detachment that hinders victims from connecting with their intuitive side and inner sensing ability.

Karl Lehman has discovered another way to focus on the heart called the Immanuel Approach (God with us).[23] He suggests you focus on a time when you felt Jesus was there for you in an image or sensation. Jesus has told us, "Surely I am with you always." (Matt. 28:20). We can then perceive the Lord's presence, connect with Him, receive with Him and just BE **with** Him. It can be powerful to focus on that visual image and allow the Holy Spirit to reveal what you really appreciate about being with Jesus.

Allowing your love tank to fill up builds a greater internal reserve—so when emotions are heightened from challenging life events, you have a greater capacity to deal with these struggles. Father Andrew Miller, Founder of Heart Sync Ministries, says, "Building intimacy with God is not a side effect, but the major goal of emotional healing."[24]

To open the heart, I like an exercise that can help people develop their intuitive side. Put your hand over your heart and take the time to remember a time when you felt very loved and appreciated. It might be with a child, an animal, a loved one, or a moment with Christ. I like to recall the time when my dear mother was dying, and her last words to me were: "I love you so much." They touched me so deeply that I use them to reinforce positive feelings about myself when I struggle. There is research to support this method called the Heart Math Institute. Sixteen years of research has proven that the heart has an intelligent memory that, if properly encouraged with loving thoughts, can overcome any negative input in our minds. I find it interesting that the scripture encourages us to guard our heart because all of life flows out of it. Proverbs 4:23 puts it this way: "Keep your heart with all diligence, for out of it spring the issues of life."

I used to struggle to make even simple decisions because I lived from my head rather than from my intuitive side. I would wrestle to decide which sunglasses to buy because I couldn't trust my preferences, worried that I would make a mistake. As a result, I ended up returning the items I had bought because I had no idea what I liked.

Since I've cleared out many of the hindrances and focused on my heart's intuition, I am much more able to hear what I need and want. Now, it's like there is a direct line between my heart and my head, and I just need to connect with the Holy Spirit to show me the way. As a result, I find it much easier to make good decisions. Ultimately, I've made it a point to stop before making purely head decisions and wait to listen and discover what my heart is saying after praying and seeking the Lord.

I've discovered that when I connect to the love of Christ on a heart level, I can clearly hear Him tell me what I need to know. With open arms, He invites us to come, but it's up to us whether to respond, making that connection to the Lord. When I stay connected with Him, it's easy to make decisions, because when I hear Him speak, I renew my mind and override any confusion or negativity that gets in my way.

Soul Searching:

1. What negative attitudes have you taken on from your family or others that deeply impact your thinking? Do they come from your upbringing or more recent situations?

2. Describe a point in time when you stayed stuck in self-pity and didn't know how to get out of a vicious downward cycle of thinking "woe is me." Share how a change of focus overcame your negative thinking.

3. Explain in detail the things you tell yourself (your self-talk) daily. Are you compassionate or condemning?

4. What steps have you taken to transform patterns of negative thinking?

Here's a great prayer you can use to speak truth to your mind. It's based on Ephesians 6:14:

"Good morning, Lord. Thank you for assuring my victory today. By faith, I choose to follow your battle plan and to prepare myself according to your instructions. In preparation for the battles I may face today, by faith I put on the belt of truth. Your Word is true. Renew my mind through the truth of your Word. Don't let me compromise your truth through my thoughts, speech, or actions. Expose in my heart the lies that I am tempted to believe. The truth is that I am your child—bought and paid for by the blood of Christ. The truth is that you love me dearly and that nothing can separate me from your love today."

Chapter Sixteen

Your Body Is a Temple

Treat your body like a temple, not a woodshed. The mind and body work together. Your body needs to be a good support system for the mind and the spirit.
—Jim Rohn

We come into this world marked by a sin nature and hereditary weaknesses that can cause us to be less than our best physically. Because of the fall, we can experience health challenges and lose hope that the Lord wants to heal us. We also live in a world that is full of toxins we take in from the chemicals in our environment and foods. Much of what our ancestors experienced of fresh, unprocessed foods and clean air is no longer available today, to say nothing of the stress that our lifestyles bring.

I believe we are to be good stewards of the bodies God has given us. We only have one body to carry us through this lifetime. And if it is truly the temple of the Holy Spirit, we must learn how to take care of it. The Bible says we may perish for lack of knowledge. I believe we need to educate ourselves about nutrition, so we understand how the body works. I am a big proponent of living a more toxin-free life, so that we don't put added stress on our bodies. I have spent hours reading nutrition books to try to sort out what is healthy for me. Even equipped with nutritional training, I've found the field to be filled with contradictory expert opinions. I've come to believe in the truth of this saying: "One man's food is another man's poison." We don't necessarily benefit from eating the same foods others can eat, due to various blood types and individual body chemistries.

Nutrition for Your Type

Authors Peter J. D'Adamo and Catherine Whitney have written an excellent book entitled *Eat Right for Your Type* that explains the foods that are best for each blood type.[25] I try to tailor my food selections to suit my blood type, keeping in mind my nutritional imbalances and food sensitivities. But in the end, I discovered that I need God's wisdom about what to eat and how to take care of myself. As I seek the Lord, He has encouraged me to eat certain healthy foods and take nutrition supplements to eliminate toxins and improve my health on a cellular level. In fact, I've made a daily habit of eating right, taking appropriate supplements, exercising and using positive thoughts to bring out the best in my body, mind, and spirit.

The way foods, especially grains, are currently refined can make them hard for people to digest, so you may find it helpful to eliminate gluten and even dairy to think clearly. The way we process grains is very inferior today. Some of us may also have genetic markers that indicate whether we can effectively handle grain. I for one, recently discovered this problem with gluten and eliminating it has made a huge improvement in my ability to heal the gut.

Not long ago I began to understand the connection between our physical and mental health and the environment of the gut. The colon is where we absorb the majority of nutrients. Researchers have recently discovered that the gut is the second brain of the body—known as the enteric nervous system (ENS). It's hard to imagine that feelings of sadness, stress, or even memory can be generated from our gut, but it's true. It manufactures over thirty neurotransmitters, including serotonin. This reference is from Dan Hurley, a science editor for gut/brain related health concerns.[26] So it's important to take care of it because out of it flow the emotions of our lives!

In the same way, dairy protein is hard for some people to break down, because of the homogenization process, which allows it to create mucus on the walls of the colon. There are plenty of non-dairy choices available today to choose from that don't have that same detrimental effect—including rice or almond milk.

Some with health challenges experience instantaneous healings—miracles. I'm always in awe when I hear the stories of the

Lord's healing work. For others, it comes as a gradual change. And if it fails to come the way we expected or when we thought it would, we dare not give up but rather trust Him to do the healing! The Lord uses the healing process to reveal underlying emotional issues or a lack of forgiveness, but it's all a part of His plan if we'll just relax and let Him work. In my case, I also see how He's increasing my understanding to help others.

Mind and Body Connection

The mind and body connection are very powerful. Our beliefs influence the kinds of chemicals that communicate with the cells of our body. And while medical practitioners hesitate to suggest an emotional component to many diseases, childhood trauma resulting in belief patterns can greatly impact our health. So, if you are struggling to believe healing is a possibility, let me put your mind at ease. The Good Shepherd has never left you and will see you through every challenge you face. Just ask for wisdom to know what you need to do at any given time because He will show you the way.

Ignoring the mind and body connection may prevent your healing. When a person is under stress due to early abuse or life events, an excess of cortisol is released into the body. Over time this creates a fight-or-flight response that begins to wear out the adrenal glands. Most abuse victims tend to have this weakness, which can take many months to repair. If we never deal with the emotional triggers that created the stress, the weakness can manifest in depression and a lack of zest for life.

I have undergone many emotional cleansings to address the issues impacting my system. When the alternative medicine practitioner diagnoses a problem, I typically go to God in prayer. I ask Him to reveal the emotional root of the issue, and when I get the answer, I take authority and command that problem or system to come into balance and heal.

I am of the opinion that it takes a combination of physical, emotional, and spiritual work to see good progress. So, when we focus on only one of the three areas, we fail to address an issue that should be approached comprehensively. Some people take every supplement in the book and end up with nothing more than expensive urine. They could even be taking the wrong supplements for their particular problem. Or they may be focused on nutrition rather than looking at the body-mind connection for healing. In the past, I made nutrition my God. The Lord revealed that I was putting far too much emphasis there, so I have learned to err on the emotional side. I know, however, that God has given us many foods that can be medicine for our bodies. We just must discern what we need at any given time.

Over the years I've discovered that if we don't get the message that is trying to get through emotionally, our bodies begin to show symptoms. The body never lies, so we need to take heed and notice the signals. For instance, compulsive eating can be an indication that we are pushing down our feelings. We may be stuffing our feelings and medicating them with food. The 12-step program that addresses this issue uses the acronym HALT and claims that we must not let the following four symptoms get out of balance. HALT stands for: hungry, angry, lonely and tired. When we are out of balance in any of these areas, we may be drawn to compulsive food urges that we're unable to control. It can be a signal that we're craving something emotionally.

It could also reflect that we are hungry for foods that feed our blood sugar when we need a temporary energy high.

> **The body never lies, so we need to take heed and notice the signals.**

Over our lifetimes, we're all prone to physical symptoms of one kind or another. We just need to trust that as we apply the principles here, we can be restored to healthy, cellular health. We must trust that the God can restore what the locust has eaten and bring us into a healthy place in mind, body, and spirit.

Soul-Searching:

1. When you think of your body as a temple of God, can you identify areas of your lifestyle or diet that are not in alignment with the care of a temple?
2. Have you been able to trust God to reveal the emotional roots of your health struggle? What stressors can you identify that affect you?
3. Do you have a daily regimen for taking care of your body? If so, what have you found effective?

Chapter Seventeen

Heaven on Earth

*God's will is simply for heaven's reality
to become earth's reality.*
—Bill Johnson

D o we have to wait until we die to experience the pleasure and well-being available in heaven? I don't believe so. If we live out the practices and principles here, it's possible to experience "heaven on earth"—no longer waiting for a physical heaven. We will never be completely whole in our physical bodies, but we can make incredible progress toward wholeness if we invite Christ into our daily lives. I believe it's possible to walk in the power of the Spirit and to experience the supernatural every day right here on earth! Despite the cat-astrophic events that happen all around us, we can rest assured that there is no fear in perfect love. Christ offers His perfect love to walk us through any difficulty we encounter. We will be protected from the effects of violence or destruction because we have a great Comforter—the Holy Spirit living inside us.

If we truly believe we can connect to God for answers, we can be free of the marks of sin that so easily entangles us, but Sunday-only Christianity rarely brings that kind of intimacy and freedom. I hope I've made it clear that it's only possible through vibrant moment-to-moment intimacy with God. Since scripture describes our hearts as deceitful, we need heart transplants every single day, which is why we need to stay connected to the Good Shepherd, who is our only access to the abundant life. Where we put our focus and whose words we heed make a vast difference. Are our eyes and ears on the lies of the enemies inside us or do we set our eyes and ears on Him? In John 5:19 Jesus explained, "I tell you the truth, the Son can do nothing by himself, but what He sees the Father do; for whatever He does, the Son also does in like manner." If we listen to what the Father tells us, we can live in full connection to the Father and live out the life He has for us: "My sheep hear my voice, and I know them, and they follow me." (John 10:27)

Open Heart Surgery

How do we do keep our hearts open and pure, so we are "living heaven on earth"? Ask God to let you see your heart as a garden on a regular basis. Ask Him to show you anything that doesn't belong in your garden—weeds, fears, anxieties or other hindrances that paralyze the development of your true authentic self—all the little traumas and negative events you encountered throughout your lifetime.

Allow time for Christ to reveal whatever is in your garden. Look around and notice everything there, asking Him to show you weeds that don't belong. You might see a root of bitterness, a lack of forgiveness toward yourself or others, or a spirit of fear that's taken you captive. Some weeds hide deep inside, and you'll need His help to see them. As you identify them, ask for His help to pull out their deep roots. As you see them uprooted one by one, watch how He transforms them into something true.

Once you allow Jesus to speak His truth into your heart, you will begin to trust His voice and see your heart transformed, completely renewed, restored as only He can. Apart from the power of the Holy Spirit, we can't untangle and free ourselves from the lies that control us. I've watched people who have struggled for years finally experience miraculous heart healing for the first time when they go to the Good Shepherd for answers. Others who doubted they would ever be healed may begin to believe that God can speak to their hearts and make all things new.

It also helps to practice gratitude daily. In order to experience the fullness of the Spirit, the scripture says: "And do not be drunk with wine, in which is dissipation, but be filled with the Spirit, speaking to one another in psalms and hymns and spiritual songs, singing and making melody in your heart to the Lord, giving thanks to God the Father in the name of our Lord Jesus Christ." (Ephesians 5:18-19)

How often do we focus on what is wrong or missing instead of thanking God for the amazing things He does for us? Research supports the fact that if we practice gratitude daily, it can positively impact our marriages, our health, and even relationships with co-workers. This new focus can change the cellular memory of our bodies! I recommend that at the end of each day you use a journal to record three things you were "being," rather than what you were "doing" to show appreciation for yourself. For example: "I was more patient with one of my difficult children." "I was loving and affectionate with my husband." This may sound foreign, but I've seen amazing results with those who used it. It goes a long way toward helping us release the "I'm not good enough" belief. Others have chosen to share one good thing that they appreciated about their mates and saw their marriage issues resolved. Practicing gratitude can rewire the neuropathways in the brain, increasing the brain's ability to experience love. How powerful is that! This new focus can change the cellular memory of our bodies and release a chemical that is a "feel good" love, a sexual hormone called oxytocin!

Take on the Full Authority

If we want to practice "heaven on earth", we need to step into the full authority Christ has given us in His Word. By using our authority, we can be set free from strongholds of fear, insecurity, scarcity, and health concerns. Strongholds are more deeply rooted beliefs that seem to take a deeper commitment to release, which is why it's important to take an active role in the process. The apostle Luke says this: "Now you understand that I have imparted to you all my authority to trample over his kingdom. You will trample upon every demon before you and overcome every power Satan possesses."(Luke 10:19) Few of us realize and take seriously that particular benefit of Christ's death, but the amazing truth is that He daily equips us to take authority over our circumstances and infirmities.

Jesus was in regular intimate communion with God, so He knew how to use that authority, doing exactly what the Father told Him to do. Before He ascended into heaven He told His disciples: "Most assuredly, I say to you, he who believes in me, the works that I do he will also do; and greater works than these he will do, because I go to My Father." (John 14:12) If we are going to do greater works, we can expect to see miracles not only outwardly, but in our hearts.

Entering the Holy of Holies

It may cost you something to live a life of connection and healing. You may feel alone and not fit in with those who are unwilling to allow Christ access to the deep recesses of their hearts. Skeptics may think you just need to stop being so intro-spective by forgetting the past and moving forward. Or you might run into those who are content to stay in their little com-fort zones of complacency and never experience transformation. You must decide if you're willing to move from the outer court into the Holy of Holies to experience all God has for you.

Before Christ's death, Levitical priests were only allowed to enter the Holy of Holies of the tabernacle once a year. On that day, called the Day of Atonement, they were to bring blood that would cover the sins of the people for the following year. But when Christ died, the veil of the temple was ripped from top to bottom, so that we now have complete access to the Holy of Holies every minute of every day, allowing us to have a full and unhindered fellowship with the King of kings! We can now boldly enter God's presence, because of the blood of Jesus. In Hebrews 6:19-20, we read: "This hope we have as an anchor of the soul, both sure and steadfast, and which enters the Presence behind the veil, where the forerunner has entered for us, even Jesus, having become High Priest forever according to the order of Melchizedek." The Holy of Holies is a representation of "heaven on earth", God's dwelling place, to which we have complete access through Christ!

When I now enter the inner court, God doesn't see my blemishes, weaknesses or issues. He sees the Son's countenance reflected on my face. He sees me as pure, forgiven, and loveable—His beloved child. We only need to draw near and put on that cloak of righteousness as we allow Him to prune away what hinders our Shalom, the place of well-being where nothing is missing or broken. It's in this place where we find what is called *Sozo*—completeness, having been saved, healed and delivered. Our awesome God's greatest desire is to restore our love connection and bring redemption, so we have access to heaven on earth.

Over the years I've discovered that it's essential to spend time alone with God. Otherwise, we will be too distracted by busyness, work responsibilities and the endless outward clamor of voices and electronic devices to make a connection with God. Jesus is our example in that He regularly left behind the crowds and even the disciples to spend time alone with God, where He was refreshed and renewed in the secret place. We too can be renewed when we take the time to retreat. I have a favorite chair where I know I will be meeting with Christ to journal, reflect on scriptures, or just sit and worship God. It allows me to enter the inner chambers of my own heart so I can more readily grasp what Christ wants me to let go. I've shared how He relentlessly pursues a relationship with us, but if we never take the time to listen, we're like empty flowerpots that grow only weeds because they've had no water. We become dry and parched because we aren't regularly receiving from the Spirit. It's in the place of daily replenishment where we live out what Jesus described as the abundant life.

> It's in the place of daily replenishment where we live out what Jesus described as the abundant life.

It's not necessarily easy to apply these principles. Scripture refers to it as the narrow way. Those who choose to take this path can find great freedom but getting there can be somewhat anxiety-ridden at times. As I look at the way He has never failed to be there to guide my steps, I'm in awe of the love and power available to me every single day! I try to look at the path, not as a destination, but as a journey that allows me to bring heaven to earth. In summary, you can access this incredible new way of life if you:

Embrace the Father's Heart for You - If we fully experience the love of the Father as a Good Shepherd, we can trust whatever comes our way.

Daily Work Out Your Salvation - It requires listening, hearing, relating, and releasing. This includes looking at unresolved emotions from your past upbringing that resulted in traumas that still impact you.

Identify Your Hindrances - Confess and repent the lies you've believed.

Allow Your Heart to Be Renewed - Renewal of the heart occurs when you leave behind beliefs that don't line up with His truth.

Develop a Heart of Gratitude - Be thankful for whatever comes your way, knowing that it is the Father's good plan to lead you into a place of great well-being, where you will reflect the character of God.

Rest in His Arms - Become equally yoked with the Father so that you can enter His rest. If you learn to truly rest, He will never leave you without His comfort and renewal. I cling tightly to the promises in Matthew 11:29-30 which says: "Come to Me, all who labor and are heavy burdened and I will give you rest. Take My yoke upon you and learn from Me, for I am gentle and humble in heart, and you will find rest for your souls. For my yoke is easy and My burden is light."

Put on the Cloak of the New Man - Allow the truth the Lord reveals to penetrate the deeper crevices in your heart.

While I haven't seen everything work out physically according to my image, I am finding myself less and less stressed when I don't feel I am where I would like to be. By giving up my self-sufficiency to make things happen I have learned that I can rest in the Lord's provisions and am able to receive more abundance from the Lord. Consequently, I have seen God bring people to me so unexpectedly that I knew it was of the Lord and not my own effort. Also, I have seen my sleep and health-related concerns greatly improve to the point where I am feeling great and ready to tackle the next phase of my life journey! And finally, being able to fully receive more of the Father's love has greatly improved being able to love and accept my husband Les. I have fallen deeper in love and respect for the man that God has developed him into!

My prayer is that you, too, find your rest in the arms of the Good Shepherd as He daily strolls through the garden of your heart hoping to take up permanent residence there. As He takes up more real estate in your heart, you can find freedom from things that prevented you from living the abundant life. I leave you with the Apostle Paul's final words: "The amazing grace of the Master, Jesus Christ, the extravagant love of God, the intimate friendship of the Holy Spirit, be with all of you." (2 Corinthians 13:14, MSG)

> The Good Shepherd daily strolls through the garden of your heart hoping to take up permanent residence there.

Soul-Searching:

1. Are you spending enough time alone with the Lord or do distractions keep you preoccupied? Share how you could make more time to spend alone with Him.

2. Imagine your heart as a garden and ask Him to show you any weeds that don't belong there.

3. What does "living heaven on earth," mean to you? Do you think it's possible to enter the Holy of Holies and live from a strong inner connection with God? If so, how will you practice that daily connection?

4. What is the main thing that you identified with as we learned about sheep? Why do you think scripture refers to us like sheep—more than 500 times? What does Christ encourage us as His sheep, to do?

5. Practice acknowledging your state of "being" vs. "doing" and notice whether you find it easy or challenging.

6. What does, "resting in the Lord," mean to you, and how can you practice more of that in your life?

7. What is the one area outlined here that you want to start applying to your life right away?

Addendum

How to Hear God's Voice—By Dr. Mark Virkler

She had done it again! Instead of coming straight home from school like she was supposed to, she had gone to her friend's house. Without permission. Without our knowledge. Without doing her chores.

With a ministering household that included remnants of three struggling families plus our own toddler and newborn, my wife simply couldn't handle all the work on her own. Everyone had to pull their own weight. Everyone had age appropriate tasks they were expected to complete. At fourteen, Rachel and her younger brother were living with us while her parents tried to overcome lifestyle patterns that had resulted in the children running away to escape the dysfunction. I felt sorry for Rachel, but honestly, my wife was my greatest concern.

Now Rachel had ditched her chores to spend time with her friends. It wasn't the first time, but if I had anything to say about it, it would be the last. I intended to lay down the law when she got home and make it very clear that if she was going to live under my roof, she would obey my rules.

But...she wasn't home yet. And I had recently been learning to hear God's voice more clearly. Maybe I should try to see if I could hear anything from Him about the situation. Maybe He could give me a way to get her to do what she was supposed to (i.e. what I wanted her to do). So, I went to my office and reviewed what the Lord had been teaching me from Habakkuk 2:1,2: "I will stand on my guard post and station myself on the rampart; And I will keep watch to see what He will speak to me... Then the Lord answered me and said, 'Record the vision....'"

Habakkuk said, "I will stand on my guard post..." (Habakkuk 2:1). **The first key to hearing God's voice is to go to a quiet place and still our own thoughts and emotions.** Psalm 46:10 encourages us to be still, let go, cease striving, and know that He is God. In Psalm 37:7 we are called to "be still before the Lord and wait patiently for Him." There is a deep inner knowing in our spirits that each of us can experience when we quiet our flesh and our minds. Practicing the art of biblical meditation helps silence the outer noise and distractions clamoring for our attention.

I didn't have a guard post but I did have an office, so I went there to quiet my temper and my mind. Loving God through a quiet worship song is one very effective way to become still. In 2 Kings 3, Elisha needed a word from the Lord so he said,

"Bring me a minstrel," and as the minstrel played, the Lord spoke. I have found that playing a worship song on my autoharp is the quickest way for me to come to stillness. I need to choose my song carefully; boisterous songs of praise do not bring me to stillness, but rather gentle songs that express my love and worship. And it isn't enough just to sing the song into the cosmos—I come into the Lord's presence most quickly and easily when I use my godly imagination to see the truth that He is right here with me and I sing my songs to Him, personally.

"I will keep watch to see," said the prophet. To receive the pure word of God, it is very important that my heart be properly focused as I become still, because my focus is the source of the intuitive flow. If I fix my eyes upon Jesus (Hebrews 12:2), the intuitive flow comes from Jesus. But if I fix my gaze upon some desire of my heart, the intuitive flow comes out of that desire. To have a pure flow I must become still and carefully fix my eyes upon Jesus. Quietly worshiping the King and receiving out of the stillness that follows quite easily accomplishes this.

So, I used **the second key to hearing God's voice: As you pray, fix the eyes of your heart upon Jesus, seeing in the Spirit the dreams and visions of Almighty God.** Habakkuk was actually looking for vision as he prayed. He opened the eyes of his heart and looked into the spirit world to see what God wanted to show him.

God has always spoken through dreams and visions, and He specifically said that they would come to those upon whom the Holy Spirit is poured out (Acts 2:1-4, 17).

Being a logical, rational person, observable facts that could be verified by my physical senses were the foundations of my life, including my spiritual life. I had never thought of opening the eyes of my heart and looking for vision. However, I have come to believe that this is exactly what God wants me to do. He gave me eyes in my heart to see in the spirit the vision and movement of Almighty God. There is an active spirit world all around us, full of angels, demons, the Holy Spirit, the omnipresent Father, and His omnipresent Son, Jesus. The only reasons for me not to see this reality are unbelief or lack of knowledge.

In his sermon in Acts 2:25, Peter refers to King David's statement: "I saw the Lord always in my presence; for He is at my right hand, so that I will not be shaken." The original psalm makes it clear that this was a decision of David's, not a constant supernatural visitation: "I have set (literally, I have placed) the Lord continually before me; because He is at my right hand, I will not be shaken." (Psalm 16:8) Because David knew that the Lord was always with him, he determined in his spirit to see that truth with the eyes of his heart as he went through life, knowing that this would keep his faith strong.

In order to see, we must look. Daniel saw a vision in his mind and said, "I was looking...I kept looking...I kept looking" (Daniel 7:2, 9, 13). As I pray, I look for Jesus, and I watch as He speaks to me, doing and saying the things that are on His heart. Many Christians will find that if they will only look, they will see. Jesus is Emmanuel, God with us (Matthew 1:23). It is as simple as that. You can see Christ present with you because Christ **is** present with you. In fact, the vision may come so easily that you will be tempted to reject it, thinking that it is just you. But if you persist in recording these visions, your doubt will soon be overcome by faith as you recognize that the content of them could only be birthed in Almighty God.

Jesus demonstrated the ability of living out of constant contact with God, declaring that He did nothing on His own initiative, but only what He saw the Father doing, and heard the Father saying (John 5:19,20,30). What an incredible way to live!

Is it possible for us to live out of divine initiative as Jesus did? Yes! We must simply fix our eyes upon Jesus. The veil has been torn, giving access into the immediate presence of God, and He calls us to draw near (Luke 23:45; Hebrews 10:19-22). "I pray that the eyes of your heart will be enlightened...."

When I had quieted my heart enough that I was able to picture Jesus without the distractions of my own ideas and plans, I was able to "keep watch to see what He will speak to me." I wrote down my question: "Lord, what should I do about Rachel?"

Immediately the thought came to me, "She is insecure." Well, that certainly wasn't my thought! Her behavior looked like rebellion to me, not insecurity.

But like Habakkuk, I was coming to know the sound of God speaking to me. (Habakkuk 2:2) Elijah described it as a still, small voice (I Kings 19:12). I had previously listened for an inner audible voice, and God does speak that way at times. However, I have found that usually, God's voice comes as spontaneous thoughts, visions, feelings, or impressions.

For example, haven't you been driving down the road and had a thought come to you to pray for a certain person? Didn't you believe it was God telling you to pray? What did God's voice sound like? Was it an audible voice, or was it a spontaneous thought that lit upon your mind?

Experience indicates that we perceive spirit-level communication as spontaneous thoughts, impressions and visions, and Scripture confirms this in many ways. For example, one definition of *paga*, a Hebrew word for intercession, is "a chance encounter or an accidental intersecting." When God lays people on our hearts, He does it through *paga*, a chance encounter thought "accidentally" intersecting our minds.

So the third key to hearing God's voice is recognizing that God's voice in your heart often sounds like a flow of spontaneous thoughts. Therefore, when I want to hear from God, I tune to chance-encounter or spontaneous thoughts.

Finally, God told Habakkuk to record the vision (Habakkuk 2:2). This was not an isolated command. The Scriptures record many examples of individual's prayers and God's replies, such as the Psalms, many of the prophets, and Revelation. I have found that obeying this final principle amplified my confidence in my ability to hear God's voice so that I could finally make living out of His initiatives a way of life. **The fourth key, two-way journaling or the writing out of your prayers and God's answers, brings great freedom in hearing God's voice.**

I have found two-way journaling to be a fabulous catalyst for clearly discerning God's inner, spontaneous flow, because as I journal I am able to write in faith for long periods of time, simply believing it is God. I know that what I believe I have received from God must be tested. However, testing involves doubt and doubt blocks divine communication, so I do not want to test while I am trying to receive. (See James 1:5-8) With journaling, I can receive in faith, knowing that when the flow has ended I can test and examine it carefully.

So I wrote down what I believed He had said: "She is insecure."

But the Lord wasn't done. I continued to write the spontaneous thoughts that came to me: "Love her unconditionally. She is flesh of your flesh and bone of your bone."

My mind immediately objected: She is not flesh of my flesh. She is not related to me at all—she is a foster child, just living in my home temporarily. It was definitely time to test this "word from the Lord"!

There are three possible sources of thoughts in our minds: ourselves, Satan and the Holy Spirit. It was obvious that the words in my journal did not come from my own mind—I certainly didn't see her as insecure or flesh of my flesh. And I sincerely doubted that Satan would encourage me to love anyone unconditionally!

Okay, it was starting to look like I might have actually received counsel from the Lord. It was consistent with the names and character of God as revealed in the Scripture, and totally contrary to the names and character of the enemy. That meant that I was hearing from the Lord, and He wanted me to see the situation in a different light. Rachel was my daughter—part of my family not by blood but by the hand of God Himself.

The chaos of her birth home had created deep insecurity about her worthiness to be loved by anyone, including me and including God. Only the unconditional love of the Lord expressed through an imperfect human would reach her heart.

But there was still one more test I needed to perform before I would have absolute confidence that this was truly God's word to me: I needed confirmation from someone else whose spiritual discernment I trusted. So, I went to my wife and shared what

I had received. I knew if I could get her validation, especially since she was the one most wronged in the situation, then I could say, at least to myself, "Thus sayeth the Lord."

Needless to say, Patti immediately and without question confirmed that the Lord had spoken to me. My entire planned lecture was forgotten. I returned to my office anxious to hear more. As the Lord planted a new, supernatural love for Rachel within me, He showed me what to say and how to say it to not only address the current issue of household responsibility, but the deeper issues of love and acceptance and worthiness. Rachel and her brother remained as part of our family for another two years, giving us many opportunities to demonstrate and teach about the Father's love, planting spiritual seeds in thirsty soil. We weren't perfect and we didn't solve all of her issues, but because I had learned to listen to the Lord, we were able to avoid creating more brokenness and separation.

The four simple keys that the Lord showed me from Habak-kuk have been used by people of all ages, from four to a hundred and four, from every continent, culture and denomination, to break through into intimate two-way conversations with their loving Father and dearest friend. Omitting any one of the keys will prevent you from receiving all He wants to say to you. The order of the keys is not important, just that you use them all. Embracing all four, by faith, can change your life. Simply quiet yourself down, tune to spontaneity, look for vision, and journal. He is waiting to meet you there.

You will be amazed when you journal! Doubt may hinder you at first, but throw it off, reminding yourself that it is a biblical concept, and that God is present, speaking to His children.

Relax. When we cease our labors and enter His rest, God is free to flow (Hebrews 4:10).

Why not try it for yourself, right now? Sit back comfortably, take out your pen and paper, and smile. Turn your attention toward the Lord in praise and worship, seeking His face. Many people have found the music and visionary prayer called "A Stroll Along the Sea of Galilee" helpful in getting them started. You can listen to it and download it free at www.CWGMinistries.org/Galilee.

After you write your question to Him, become still, fixing your gaze on Jesus. You will suddenly have a very good thought. Don't doubt it; simply write it down. Later, as you read your journaling, you, too, will be blessed to discover that you are indeed dialoguing with God. If you wonder if it is really the Lord speaking to you, share it with your spouse or a friend. Their input will encourage your faith and strengthen your commitment to spend time getting to know the Lover of your soul more intimately than you ever dreamed possible.

Is It Really God?

Five ways to be sure what you're hearing is from Him:

1) Test the Origin (1 John 4:1)

Thoughts from our own minds are progressive, with one thought leading to the next, however tangentially. Thoughts from the spirit world are spontaneous. The Hebrew word for true prophecy is *naba*, which literally means to bubble up, whereas false prophecy is *ziyd* meaning to boil up. True words from the Lord will bubble up from our innermost being; we don't need to cook them up ourselves.

2) Compare It to Biblical Principles

God will never say something to you personally which is contrary to His universal revelation as expressed in the Scriptures. If the Bible clearly states that something is a sin, no amount of journaling can make it right. Much of what you journal about will not be specifically addressed in the Bible, however, so an understanding of biblical principles is also needed.

3) Compare It to the Names and Character of God as Revealed in the Bible

Anything God says to you will be in harmony with His essential nature. Journaling will help you get to *know* God personally, but knowing what the Bible says *about* Him will help you discern what words are from Him. Make sure the tenor of your journaling lines up with the character of God as described in the names of the Father, Son and Holy Spirit.

4) Test the Fruit (Matthew 7:15-20)

What effect does what you are hearing have on your soul and your spirit? Words from the Lord will quicken your faith and increase your love, peace and joy. They will stimulate a sense of humility within you as you become more aware of who God is and who you are. On the other hand, any words you receive which cause you to fear or doubt, which bring you into confusion or anxiety, or which stroke your ego (especially if you hear something that is "just for you alone—no one else is worthy") must be immediately rebuked and rejected as lies of the enemy.

5) Share It with Your Spiritual Counselors (Proverbs 11:14)

We are members of a Body! A cord of three strands is not easily broken and God's intention has always been for us to grow together. Nothing will increase your faith in your ability to hear from God like having it confirmed by two or three other people! Share it with your spouse, your parents, your friends, your elder, your group leader, even your grown children can be your sounding board. They don't need to be perfect or super-spiritual; they just need to love you, be committed to being available to you, have a solid biblical orientation, and most importantly, they must also willingly and easily receive counsel. Avoid the authoritarian who insists that because of their standing in the church or with God, they no longer need to listen to others. Find two or three people and let them confirm that you are hearing from God!

The book *4 Keys to Hearing God's Voice* is available at www.CWGMinistries.org.

Acknowledgments

I give special acknowledgment to Morgan James Publishing Company for their excellent expertise and support in the publishing of this book.

I was greatly encouraged by my dear friend Carol Johnson who volunteered her time to "book storm" with me to get clarity on my vision and target reader. Her sessions with me were invaluable.

I give special acknowledgment to Terri Parzybok with Living Free Ministries for her continued encouragement to me in understanding and embracing the Father's love. Her loving me through some diffcult times has had an impact on my life and family. Through her ministry, I learned many wonderful healing principles that have made my journey beneficial.

I was appreciative of the time spent in a writing circle with Janice Shannon. We were able to have other eyes on our writing that was very helpful.

I acknowledge the talented editing ability of Nancy Arant Williams (www.nancyarantwilliams.com) who caught the vision for the manuscript and captured my message so beautifully.

I am grateful for the skillful grammar ability of Sue Carter as she worked with me in the initial stages to give me pointers and was able to use her excellent proofreading skills to bring this manuscript to fruition. I appreciated some additional help with editing from Sylvia Wright and Sarah Thiessen.

Meet the Author

Suzanne began exploring her passion for healing the mind/body and spirit at a young age. She has since been led to many alternative means that bring restoration to the body and soul. Her yearning for growing in her relationship with the Lord and wanting others to experience all they can have spiritually led her to convey these words. She shares opening her own journey along with others as she poured out the healing principles she has learned on pages of this book.

She is a Licensed Professional Counselor, Board Certified Life Coach, Nutritionist, and speaker. Over several decades of personal experience, she has attained a wide range of expertise to draw from in her toolbox. She is a Master Certified Splankna practitioner through the Splankna Therapy Institute. She spent multiple years coaching with Tony Robbins Research International, where she learned some cutting-edge strategies to bring change by moving past limitations in one's life. In addition, she has been affiliated with various Christian ministries and non-profits through the years.

She longs to ignite people to a deeper more whole, healthy life. Her blog *Renewed Life* (which can be located on her website) shares transformational inspirations on growing in understanding of the growth process. She and her husband Les continue to desire to relate what's possible with a surrendered heart.

In addition to this book she has written a workbook titled *Winning the Inner Game: Moving from Defeat to Victory God's Way.*

Find Suzanne on her website at
www.renewedlifecounseling.com.

This book can best be applied as you work through the soul-searching questions either individually or with a small group and facilitator.

Some of these ideas are somewhat radical ideas from traditional therapeutic methods. Suzanne welcomes any feedback through email on how this book has helped your healing process.

How to Work with Suzanne...
• One-on-one emotional healing sessions
(either in person or through long distance with Skype)
• Group teleclasses
• Inner prayer ministry sessions
• Life coaching
Bonus Freebies:
Free ebook available
on the website www.renewedlifecounseling.com
entitled *8 Strategies to Stop Self-Sabotage*.

Awakening Your Heart to More Loving:
Stress Relief Exercises for your Daily Ritual.

Contact Suzanne to assess your readiness to work together
suzanne@renewedlifecounseling.com
www.renewedlifecounseling.com
facebook.com/renewedlifecounseling

Endnotes

Chapter 1: Cracking the Wall

1   Lewis, C.S., www.cslewis.com/us/.

Chapter 2: The Good Shepherd

2   Frost, Jack, *Experiencing Father's Embrace*. Shippensburg, PA: Destiny Image Publishers Inc., 2002.

3   Keller, W. Phillip, A Shepherd Looks at Psalm 23. Grand Rapids, MI: Zondervan Publishing House, 1970.

Chapter 3: Broken Cisterns

4   Manning, Brennan, *Abba's Child: The Cry of the Heart for Intimate Belonging*. Colorado Springs, CO: NavPress Publishing Group, 1994. 51.

Chapter 5: Making Friends with Feelings

5   Brown, Brené, *Daring Greatly: How the Courage to Be Vulnerable Transforms the Way We Live, Love, Parent, and Lead*. London, England: Gotham Books: a member of Penguin Books Inc. 2012. 131-132, 138.

6   Truman, Karol, *Feelings Alive Never Die*. St. George, Utah: Olympus Distributing, 1991, 2003.

7   Branden, Nathaniel, *The Six Pillars of Self-Esteem*. New York, NY: Bantam Books, 1994.

Chapter 7: Are Your Ready and Willing?

8   Smith, Ed, www.transformation-prayer.org.

9   Thiessen, Sarah J., Splankna: *The Redemption of Energy Healing for the Kingdom of God*. Rockwall, TX: Cross House Publishing, 2011.

Chapter 8: Trauma Moments

10 Wilder, James E., and Frieson, James G., Bierling, Anne, Koepcke, Rick, and Poole, Meredith, *Living from the Heart Jesus Gave You*. East Peoria, IL.: Shepherd's House, Inc., 2013. 42-46.

11 Lipton, Bruce, *The Biology of Belief: Unleashing the Power of Consciousness, Power, and Miracles*. Carlsbad, CA: Hay House, Inc., 2005.

12 Pert, Candace B., *Molecules of Emotion*. New York, NY: Touchtone Rockefeller Center, 1997.

13 Sylvia, Claire and Novak, William, *A Change of Heart*. New York, NY: Warner Books, Inc., 1997.

14 Wentz, Marilyn Bay, and Bay, Mildred Nelson, *All We Like Sheep: Lessons from the Sheepfold*. Greeley, CO: Cladach Publishing, 2015. 93.

15 Hetland, Leif, *Baptism of Love*, Peachtree, GA: Global Mission Awareness, 2012. 63.

Chapter 9: Letting Go

16 Eddy, Lee, www.crossandswordministries.com—contributor of the courtyard exercise.

Chapter 10: When the Physical Doesn't Work

17 Hurnard, Hannah, *Hinds Feet for High Places*. London, England: Tyndale House Publishers, 1975. 214.

Chapter 11: Storms of Life

18 Sorge, Bob, *Between the Lines: God is Writing Your Story*. Grandview, MO: Oasis House, 2012.

19 Adams, Barry, *Father's Love Letter*, copyright© 1999, 2003 Father Heart Communications, www.FathersLoveLetter.com

Chapter 15: A Renewed Mind

20 Leaf, Caroline, *Switch on Your Brain: The Key to Peak Happiness, Thinking, and Health*. Grand Rapids, MI.: Baker Books, 2013.

21 Craig, Gary, Emotional Freedom Technique (EFT), www.emofree.com.

22 Neff, Kristen, *Stop Beating Yourself Up and Leave Insecurity Behind*. New York, NY: William Morrow, 2011.

23 Lehman, Dr. Karl, www.immauelapproach.com

24 Miller, Father Andrew, www.HeartSyncMinistries.org

Chapter 16: Your Body Is a Temple
25 D'Adamo, Dr. Peter J. with Whitney, Catherine, *Eat Right for Your Type: The Individualized Diet Solution to Staying Healthy, Living Longer & Achieving Your Ideal Weight.* New York, NY: G. P. Putnam's Sons, 1996.
26 Hurley, Dan, "Your Backup Brain," Psychology Today, November, 2011.

Resources

Dr. Josh Axe, www.draxe.com. The website contains extensive information about health ailments, wellness, and essential oils.

Buchan, Tamara, various resources on identity at www.ReclaimInitiative.com and Bible study series *You Were Meant for More*.

Heart Math Institute, www.heartmath.org. Extensive research on the heart connection for stress relief.

Emotional Freedom Technique resources are found at: www.glorywaves.org/product/eft-for-christians-ebook

Kayembe, Charity Virkler and Virkler, Mark, *Hearing God Through Your Dreams: Understanding the Language God Speaks at Night*. This is a great book on dreams with ideas about quantum physics woven in. www.glorywaves.org/product/

Lehman, Dr. Karl, www.immauelapproach.com. Dr. Lehman teaches how to experience an "Immanuel moment" of imaging Jesus being in a positive place of appreciation.

Mercola, Dr. Joseph, www.mercola.com. This a great website for any health-related issue.

Miller, Father Andrew, www.HeartSyncMinistries.org. A guided inner prayer ministry that brings synchronization to divided areas of the heart.

Richards, Jim, Impact Ministries, www.impactministries.com, menu. Making the Journey/ Biblical EFT video.

Sozo Ministry, www.bethelsozo.com. Sozo is an inner healing ministry that gets to the root of what hinders one's connection to Father, Son, and Holy Spirit.

Virkler, Mark, *Hearing God's Voice* DVD's and Addendum, www.cwgministries.org.